g⬤lf
CROSSWORDS

Matt Gaffney

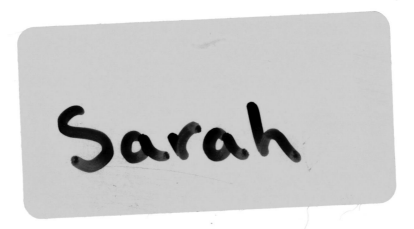

Sarah

Sterling Publishing Co., Inc.
New York

2 4 6 8 10 9 7 5 3 1

Published by Sterling Publishing Co., Inc.
387 Park Avenue South, New York, NY 10016
© 2004 by Matt Gaffney
Distributed in Canada by Sterling Publishing
℅ Canadian Manda Group, 165 Dufferin Street
Toronto, Ontario, Canada M6K 3H6
Distributed in Great Britain by Chrysalis Books Group PLC
The Chrysalis Building, Bramley Road, London W10 6SP, England
Distributed in Australia by Capricorn Link (Australia) Pty. Ltd.
P.O. Box 704, Windsor, NSW 2756, Australia

Printed in China

Sterling ISBN 1-4027-0545-X

CONTENTS

INTRODUCTION

More than other sports, golf is a producer of good stories. A pickup basketball game might yield a memorable blocked shot, and an afternoon's tennis match may be highlighted by an ace or volley that will later be recalled with pride. But a few hours on the links is likely to yield not just a bit of a tan, but also a decent yarn or two, and golf anecdotes indeed seem to be among the most entertaining in the sporting world. The cause for this is likely the amount of quiet, non-athletic time spent during a round of golf, during which we humans have occasion to act, react, and quip in memorable, humorous ways.

My own best golf story took place at the East Potomac Park golf course in Washington, D.C., a few years ago. My brother, Sean, and I had gone out to play 18 holes one bright Sunday morning, and were matched up with two solo players, Larry and Bob. Larry was an outgoing guy, sporting a fedora, introducing himself with a smile, and joking constantly about his lousy golf skills ("Let's see if I can put this one into the parking lot" is a line I recall).

Bob, on the other hand, was extremely quiet and reserved, and didn't say a single word to us—literally—after awkwardly introducing himself. If Sean, Larry, or I said "nice shot," he'd just nod without any expression. After a few holes we stopped trying to initiate any kind of contact with him.

Then, on the sixteenth hole, after a wordless morning, Bob blossomed. Larry, Sean, and I were grouped closely on the left edge of the fairway, waiting for Bob to shoot from the right side of the fairway, perhaps twenty yards from us. Bob took a mighty swing, but topped his shot badly, and the ball skittered six or seven yards into a sand trap.

And suddenly Bob, who had not spoken all day, screamed, and I mean screamed, a certain four-letter word that's best not yelled in public. As the word resonated across the course, Larry, Sean, and I looked at each other in disbelief, and other groups at neighboring holes looked over as well.

Unperturbed, Bob ambled up to the sand trap, lined up his shot—and got a ton of sand, but very little ball. It rolled a few feet but never really had a shot at leaving the bunker.

And again Bob screamed, and I mean screamed, another naughty four-letter word.

He didn't say another word the rest of the day. I suppose all the round's frustrations had left his body with those two shouted syllables, proving Ray Floyd's quip that "they call it golf because all the other four-letter words were taken."

Hopefully this book of 72 golf-themed crosswords (one for each hole in a four-day tournament!) won't prove as frustrating as Bob's day on the links. There are no sand traps in this volume, after all, and besides, the answers are in the back.

—Matt Gaffney

THE ROARING '20S

The decade in golf.

ACROSS

1 Golf shoe feature
5 Snack bar seasoning
9 Lion's hands
13 Phoenix ___
14 Links obstruction
15 Breaks, as a putter over one's knee
17 He won back-to-back PGA Championships, 1928–29
19 Alaskan shelter
20 Scorecard number
22 Famed English prep school attended by James Bond
23 Andrew and Paul: Abbr.
26 LPGA Tour player Leigh ___ Mills
27 Senior PGA Tour player Doyle and namesakes
29 Scorecard sums
31 ___ Skins Game
33 "You ___ Sunshine"
34 ___ mashie (six-iron)
35 Ball's fairway bounce
38 "Haven't ___ you somewhere?"

39 Article on pgatour.com
40 Quigley on the links
41 Md. neighbor
42 Arachnophobia and agoraphobia
43 +1 result
44 Like golfing, to some
46 ___-one
47 First player to win over $1.75 million in a year on the Tour
49 Bovine comment
50 Dir. on a compass
51 United ___ Emirates (home to the Dubai Creek golf course)
52 Pennsylvania course that's hosted seven U.S. Opens

56 Decathlon champ Johnson
58 Event first held in 1922
62 George Jetson's dog
63 Cleveland's lake
64 Mercedes or Buick
65 Exxon, in Canada
66 Went way down in the rankings
67 Tiny noise

DOWN

1 Guffawing, in Internet lingo
2 Copy
3 Mark McCormack, for example
4 Plays the 18th
5 Yacht backs
6 You're breathing a small amount of it right now

7 Soup vegetable
8 Prefix with vision
9 "___ Love You"
10 San ___, TX
11 Captain of the first U.S. Ryder Cup team, 1927
12 3-wood, in the old days
16 "My Three ___"
18 Home to PGA European Tour player Massimo Florioli
21 First name of the 1988 Masters champ
23 Very serious
24 Singer known as "The Velvet Fog"
25 In 1926 the USGA legalized clubs with these
28 It might be tight
30 Abbr. on an invoice

31 It may be asexual
32 They're good listeners
34 Musial or Getz
36 ___ a million
37 First name of the 1999 U.S. Open winner
39 "___ evil"
40 U.S. currency: Abbr.
42 Country that's home to the famous golf clubs Pau and Hardelot: Abbr.
43 Frontiersman Daniel
45 Glowers in the fireplace
46 Sent a shot to the left, maybe
47 Dr. Zhivago's love
48 Delete
49 Year when Tiger Woods will turn 77, in Roman numerals
53 Leaves stunned
54 Marx or Rove
55 Wedge locale
57 Aussie marsupial, slangily
59 Actor's signal
60 Western Indian
61 Madonna's genre of music

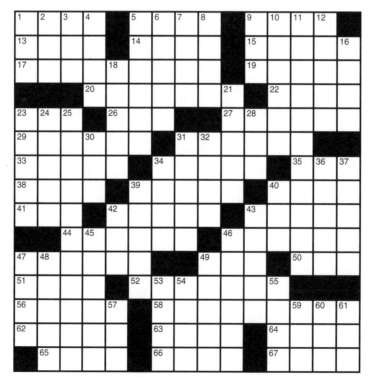

ANSWER, PAGE 79

THE 59ERS

Members of a very exclusive golf club.

ACROSS

1 ___ Caribbean Classic
6 He shot a 59 in the 1991 Las Vegas Invitational
10 Muscles targeted by crunches
13 Irish standard "Goodnight, ___"
14 Buffalo's lake
15 Beat a retreat
16 He shot a 59 in the 1998 Nike Dominion Open on the Nike Tour
18 Site of the Taj Mahal
19 Jupiter neighbor
20 Organ near the stomach
22 One of the Beverly Hillbillies
25 Part of Q&A
26 Looks over the story
27 Shot ___ of 72 (made par for the day)
29 Rub elbows
32 "Golfer," "bogey," and "Jack Nicklaus"

33 Where Babe Zaharias and Kathy Whitworth were born
34 Tony Jacklin's nat.
37 Small advantage
38 Made a chip shot
39 Plains Indian
40 Mr. Tryba
41 Kind of closet
42 Kind of musical composition associated with Bach
43 One of Tiger's 2000 triumphs
45 Metric measurements
46 Pebble Beach Golf ___
48 Cart ___
49 Fish eggs
50 Looks forward to
52 Said
53 ___ a mulligan

54 He shot a 59 in the final round to win the 1999 Bob Hope Chrysler Classic
60 Consumer
61 Greek god of war
62 Golden Globe–winning role for Madonna
63 Vocalize
64 Triplett who won the 2000 Nissan Open
65 Thomas Bjorn and compatriots

DOWN

1 ___ Tin Tin
2 Gold, south of the border
3 Up to this point
4 Santa ___, Calif.
5 Tom and family
6 Clubhouse orders
7 Work units

8 George Bush once headed it
9 Location of some Florida courses
10 He shot a 59 in the 1977 Memphis Classic
11 French artist's topper
12 Golfers Murphy and Pappas
15 Back-to-back Masters winner
17 R.E.M. or U2
21 Autograph seekers carry them
22 1982 U.S. Women's Open winner ___ Alex
23 Deteriorate
24 He shot a 59 in the 1998 Nike Valley Open on the Nike Tour
28 One, to the French

29 LPGA Tour player Alfredsson
30 Beasts of burden
31 Like some lies
33 Stereo knob
35 Prefix with surgery
36 Golf course birds
38 Cool
39 Players like to make it at tournaments
41 Went down in match play
42 Got together, as a Ryder Cup team
44 Rockies athlete
45 Three-stroke advantage, for example
46 Wide: Latin
47 "___ Teen-age Werewolf"
48 Search a person
51 Pierre's state: Abbr.
52 ___ par
55 Bush ex-spokesman Fleischer
56 School founded by Thomas Jefferson
57 Sportscaster Scully
58 Lunched
59 Spanish article

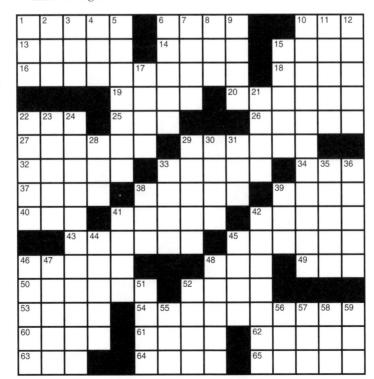

ANSWER, PAGE 80

7

WORKING THE SWING SHIFT

Some of golf's great coaches.

ACROSS

1 The U.S. Women's Open, say
6 Make it up as you go along
11 3, 4, or 5, usually
14 In reserve
15 Part of Louisiana
16 Prefix with metric
17 Used a stopwatch
18 PGA Tour tournament
19 Teachers' org.
20 Hats for Payne Stewart
21 Speaker's platform
22 Make it past, as a water hazard
24 Britannica vol.
25 1957 Masters champ Doug
26 They may be made of cedar
27 Beautiful woman
29 Milk, to Sergio Garcia
31 Earthquake shake
33 Jazz singer Fitzgerald

34 Let 'er ___ (take a big swing)
37 Like ball washers
38 Is facing, as a shot
39 Horse-controllers
41 Score-keeping tool
42 ___ solid perfect (like a great golf shot)
44 Driving sounds
45 Part of a grip
46 Golf, for Tour players
47 One of the Tours
50 Welsh form of "John"
52 ___ Paulo, Brazil
55 More based in reality
56 Pipe part
57 Exclude
58 Neither Dem. nor Rep.
59 Prepare parmesan, perhaps

61 "___ Called Wanda"
62 It may be downhill
63 Rarin' to go
64 Champion's possession
65 "___ Misérables"
66 Gets close
67 Common anesthetic

DOWN

1 Dull finish
2 Another one of the Tours
3 Coach who runs golf academies across the country
4 Poems that praise
5 Color of some tees
6 "Fuzzy Wuzzy was ___"
7 Coach who wrote "The Golf Swing"

8 Soap ingredients
9 Charged particle
10 Tiger's vaunted coach
11 Torrey ___ Golf Course (site of the Buick Invitational)
12 "Have ___!"
13 Crowd sounds
21 Gloomy
23 Elder of golf
25 Coach who Hal Sutton credits for his career's resurgence
26 250, to Tacitus
28 Baseball caller
30 See 48-Down
31 Recipe amt.
32 Wade opponent
34 He's coached Lee Janzen, Vijay Singh, and Phil Mickelson
35 Contract liquid

36 Letter afterthoughts
38 Actor who overacts
40 Home to the anvil and hammer
43 Ger., Fra., etc.
44 Did a few laps
45 Halved hole
47 Like respectful fans while a player is shooting
48 With 30-Down, 1994 and 1997 U.S. Open champ
49 Some sculptures
51 Keeps to the right, maybe
53 Supermarket section
54 "None of the above" relative
56 Long tale
57 "What do you make ___?"
60 Football's Carruth
61 Chowed down

ANSWER, PAGE 82

HAVING A BALL

And learning about them, too.

ACROSS

1 Former LPGA player Jessen
5 Part of an iron head
10 Langer's country: Abbr.
13 "___ it!" (ball-searcher's yell)
14 ___ rules (some course guidelines)
15 Fisherman's bait
16 Soft-covered flier used by most Tour players
18 Big name in shaving
19 Golf cap feature
20 Cooked lightly in butter
22 Make a difference
25 Faxon and others
26 They're in a pride
27 Ball hit into the water, say
30 Over par
31 "I'll leave ___ you"
33 Key on a computer
36 That lady's
37 Amazingly, material golf balls were once made of
38 "Interview With the Vampire" actor
39 Wood used for some woods
40 Dozing
41 Give the once-over
42 Part of USGA
44 Prefix with centrism
45 "Are too!" comeback
47 Command from a superior
48 Late flight
50 Please, in Potsdam
52 Tiger's dad
53 Early balls that gave us the term "birdie"
58 Some poetry
59 Swedish bombshell
60 Cable channel that airs golf news
61 Actor Beatty
62 Lewis and Long
63 Pool table edge

DOWN

1 Tease gently
2 1999 Ryder Cup champs
3 ___ Aviv
4 "My goodness!"
5 Shot out of the sand
6 Wolf: Spanish
7 Rent-___
8 Tex. city
9 Building wings
10 Golf ball material made from the Malaysian sapodilla plant
11 Made a mistake
12 Tries to figure out a putt
15 LPGA Tour star Davies
17 Spastic movements
21 More than dislike
22 First letter, to some
23 Tools for escaping prisoners
24 Approximate number of dimples on most golf balls
27 Produced offspring
28 Mickey Spillane's "___ Jury"
29 Walking unit
31 School worry
32 Mr. Irwin
34 Penn and Young
35 Silent watercraft
37 Everyone but the clergy
41 Helmsman
43 Christmas carols
44 Ending for major
45 "Your lights ___"
46 Winner at Gettysburg
47 One of the Three Musketeers
49 D-I links
50 Lacking clothing
51 Play ___ ear (improvise)
54 Water, to Haitians
55 "This ___ travesty!"
56 Prefix with center
57 Lorne Michaels's show, for short

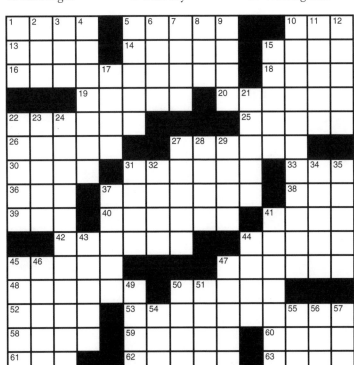

ANSWER, PAGE 84

HISTORY LESSON

Black history on the links.

ACROSS

1 Flagstick's home
5 Advice on one's grip, for instance
8 "I'm just as good ___!"
13 Highbrow musical entertainment
15 Tool for gardeners
16 Golfers like it low
17 First black winner of a PGA Tour event, 1964's Waco Open
19 Get, as a 16-Across
20 Shoo-___ (easy victors)
21 Golfer who once shot −36
23 Point ___ return
24 Fellow
25 "Much ___ About Nothing"
27 Golfer who pressured the PGA into lifting the "Caucasian race" clause barring blacks from the Tour
35 "Let ___!"
36 Made in ___ (like some golf clubs)
37 ___-putt
38 Have ___ on (be guaranteed to win)

40 Org. that preceded the CIA
41 Sportscaster Cohn
43 Q trailers
44 Company known for making drums
47 You might see one on a golf course early in the morning
48 First black player allowed to compete on the PGA Tour
51 Female barnyard resident
52 Kind of painting
53 Player of golf
56 Society's no-nos
60 A caddy carries it
63 Texas structure
65 2nd place finisher at the Senior PGA Tour's 2001 MasterCard Championship

67 ___ up (prepared a putt)
68 "Saturday Night Live" alum Gasteyer
69 Have a longing
70 Arrangement for some who acquire autos
71 Golf shop big shot: Abbr.
72 Classic cars

DOWN

1 Indian tribe of Arizona
2 Nissan ___
3 ___ through (allows a faster group by)
4 Before, to poets
5 God for whom a day of the week is named
6 Des Moines's state

7 Ivy League school, for short
8 Balaam's animal, in the Bible
9 PGA Qualifying ___
10 Horse's foot
11 5-___
12 "Take ___ your leader!"
14 Pop star Paula
18 "Don't ___ in!"
22 ___ in for birdie
24 Voting segment
26 Use an old phone
27 Like Ian Woosnam
28 "___ birdie!" (golf course cry)
29 "Oh, give me ___ ..."
30 Southwest sights
31 Food for Tommy Nakajima
32 Solitary sort
33 Wound up

34 Backside
35 French PGA European Tour player ___ Farry
39 "Twin Peaks" actor MacLachlan
42 Tiger, to many young golfers
45 "___ Misbehavin'"
46 "He's got about ___ left for par" (golf announcer's line)
49 "Vijay" and "Begay," and similar pairs
50 Like some hole-in-one claims
53 Nerve
54 "I cannot tell ___"
55 ___ close second (almost won)
57 In ___ (stuck)
58 Crosby of golf fame
59 Texas golfer Uresti
60 Scottish hillside
61 Like ___ (with skill)
62 Top army brass: Abbr.
64 Form of poetry
66 "___ the ramparts ..."

ANSWER, PAGE 86

WHAT A YEAR!

Four with an annus mirabilis.

ACROSS

1 Dropped from the leader board
6 Dir. for navigators
9 Women of the house
14 Get ___ out of (provoke)
15 Indulgent sigh
16 Ready to throw one's putter into the pond
17 He won the Masters and British Open in 1990
19 Ohio city
20 Day three of most PGA Tour events: Abbr.
21 Time of dominance
22 Cash dispenser
24 Mess tent workers, for short
25 He said he never watched Hogan's swing
27 Ritz rival
29 ___ PG-13 (like "Happy Gilmore")
32 Unwelcome nibblers
34 Don of the radio
37 Part of USGA
39 Prefix with par
40 Mr. Le Pew
41 Like John Daly
42 Golf book feature

45 Nutty ___ fruitcake
46 Thing
48 Bird from Australia
49 Mr. Clarke on the links
51 Drug cop
52 Crowd's reaction to a missed two-footer
54 "Ode to a Nightingale" poet
55 Ardena, to Vijay Singh
57 Like some events on the Golf Channel
59 Bovine word
61 Shout in a bullring
63 Some univ. employees
64 Mr. Sutton
67 Church singers
69 He won the PGA Championship and the British Open in 1994
72 Pete's rival on the tennis court
73 Dr. of rap
74 Broadcast sound
75 ___ out (barely beats)
76 Actor Mineo of "Rebel Without a Cause"
77 Oboists need them

DOWN

1 Gallery members
2 Solo song
3 Book by Noah Webster: Abbr.
4 Alaskan lang.
5 Played to keep, as a title
6 Greeting at the Dubai Desert Classic
7 Down in the dumps
8 "Hold on a sec!"
9 Sunny city to golf in
10 Noah had one
11 He won the Masters and British Open in 1998
12 Heading, as the leader board
13 D.C. has 100: Abbr.
18 "These Guys ___ Good!" (PGA slogan)
23 Part of a Clint Eastwood title
25 Golf bag contents
26 Emotion felt after a lousy shot
28 Joint that's a key part of a golf stance
29 Constantly remind someone of, as a loss
30 Soul singer Baker
31 He won the British Open, U.S. Open, and PGA Championship in 2000
33 Mixed-breed dog
35 Shocking win
36 Penn and Young
38 Leo who twice won the PGA Championship
43 Org. for doctors
44 Doesn't birdie, doesn't bogey
47 Sprint rival
50 ___ tees
53 Package at the post office
56 Links warnings
58 Korean golf sensation
59 Thom of footwear
60 Shout as your ball is heading for the water
62 Comes to a halt
64 Seek cover
65 Amino or hydrochloric
66 Some people born in August
68 Extreme anger
70 Component of many nest eggs
71 Wish one hadn't

ANSWER, PAGE 88

11

MADE IN JAPAN

Tales from the Far East.

ACROSS

1 1981 and 1989 PGA Tour leading money-winner
5 Jack who ate no fat
10 It's dimpled in Florida—but it's not a golf ball
14 Biblical murder victim
15 Longingly wish (for)
16 PGA Tour player Wayne
17 Tour event sponsored by a Japanese company
19 Surrounding regions
20 Part of ETA
21 Inadvisable tactics
22 Nicholas and Nicholas II
23 ___ Antonio
24 Men of the house, for short
25 He was zapped by St. Andrews's Road Hole on the brink of winning the 1978 British Open
32 Country where you can play at the Los Inkas Golf Club
33 It runs a golf cart
34 Baseball legend Ty
36 Was strokes up
37 "The ___ on the Shore"
38 "Gotcha!"
39 Takes to court
41 They were spent in Naples

43 Black bird
44 Position of Yoshiro Mori, who was criticized for continuing his round of golf even after learning of the sinking of a Japanese fishing vessel by a U.S. submarine
47 Do some groundskeeping work
48 ___ birdie (like some putts)
49 Club features
52 Doesn't do a thing
55 "Beat it!"
58 Howard and Hextall
59 He won his 100th worldwide tournament in 1996

61 Patron saint of sailors
62 More cool under pressure
63 "___ her on a Monday ..."
64 Day or Hnatiuk of the Tour
65 Won at chess
66 Mexican moolah

DOWN

1 Canadian LPGA Tour player Lorie
2 Sacred bird of the Nile
3 Crossword puzzle, in a sense
4 Countryman of Goosen
5 Double eagle, vis-à-vis albatross
6 Exploited laborer
7 At full attention
8 Warmongering god

9 Spike TV's former name
10 Honda ___
11 Sister and wife of Zeus
12 State for the court
13 "Buenos ___" (greeting from Olazabal)
18 Aussie star ___ Scott
22 ___ Mahal
23 Where Payne Stewart played college golf
24 ___ for the course
25 Prepare to use a driver
26 Playing ___
27 "___ in trouble!" (comment when you've just hooked a shot through a clubhouse window)

28 Video golf company
29 Holy book, for about a billion
30 Dudley of "Arthur"
31 Find loathsome
32 It may come before "thx"
35 Acknowledge the gallery theatrically
40 1987 U.S. Open champ Scott
41 1947 U.S. Open champ Worsham
42 Pioneering Charlie in golf
43 Headquarters: Abbr.
45 Parts of yrs.
46 Nothing special
49 Great White Shark's name
50 Move toward the cup
51 "She Believes ___" (Kenny Rogers song)
52 ___ Brasi ("The Godfather" character who "sleeps with the fishes")
53 Exclude
54 Have ___ in one's bonnet
55 Golf, after all
56 Eisenhower and Turner
57 Drummer Puente
59 Mr. Furyk
60 Close the pocket on one's golf bag

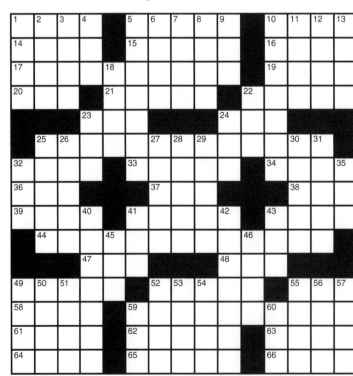

ANSWER, PAGE 90

ALL-AMERICAN BOYS

Testing your college knowledge.

ACROSS

1 One brick shy of a load
6 ___ rules (what govern some courses)
11 ___ Hill Invitational
14 Alternative
15 Home of the University of Maine
16 ___ grecque (cooked in olive oil)
17 Where Bill Glasson was an All-American
19 It goes with neither
20 Welsh golf star of the 1940s and '50s ___ Rees
21 Night shiner
22 Bus coin
24 Ankle trouble
27 Love, to Lucretius
28 Where Rick Fehr was an All-American
34 Johnny Cash's "___ the Line"
37 Fisherman's gear
38 D.C. arguer, for short
39 Graf rival
40 Clear ___ bell

41 Contemporary coffee
43 Wee
44 Part of a process
45 Norway's greatest playwright
46 Where Dan Forsman was an All-American
50 Nancy Lopez or Annika Sorenstam, once
51 Three-time major winner Larry
55 In ___ (fit)
57 Catch sight of, as a ball in the rough
60 Point opposite WSW
61 On a streak
62 Where David Duval was an All-American
66 Lennon loved her
67 Gawking type

68 "My Cousin Vinny" Oscar winner Marisa
69 Yards ___ drive
70 Wild West "necktie"
71 The Road Runner often zips past them

DOWN

1 Golf bag choices
2 In ___ (ready for a sand wedge)
3 Lead the tournament committee
4 ___ Nagle (Aussie who won the 1960 British Open)
5 Scottish star Gary
6 Wolf, to Jimenez
7 Famed Nabisco product

8 Navajo staple
9 Creature much smaller than a golf ball
10 "I ___ ball" (course lament)
11 Sends to the poorhouse
12 ___ vera
13 Improbable story, like how your buddy eagled a hole while playing in Madagascar
18 Prefix with present
23 Tic-tac-toe victory
25 Possessing the skills
26 Bugs
27 Morning times, for short
29 Persona non ___
30 Greenskeepers use them

31 Make adjustments in one's game
32 Take heed of
33 Scottish site
34 Mallorca o Ibiza
35 Mike on the links
36 One reason not to search for your ball near the water in Florida
41 Word in many food names
42 Genesis victim
44 Adam "Happy Gilmore" Sandler's old show: Abbr.
47 Nada
48 Portland's place
49 Arguing against
52 Comes across as
53 ___ year (Masters frequency)
54 Some sodas
55 Pro ___
56 Improve, as putting skill
57 ___ round
58 Golfer Ford, Bush, or Clinton: Abbr.
59 Horribly uncouth fellow
63 It may be crushed on the course
64 Cash source
65 Foot feature

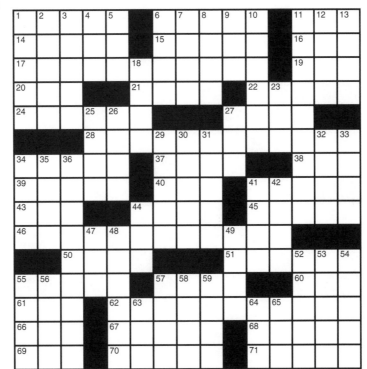

MM NUMBERS

Leaders of the year 2000.

ACROSS

1 Ms. Alcott
4 With 8-Across, 2000 PGA Tour leader in putting, with just 1.704 putts per hole
8 See 4-Across
13 ___ double take (look again)
14 Radar O'Reilly's state
15 Like golf courses at sunrise
16 2000 PGA Tour leader in driving distance, with 301.4 yards per drive
18 ___ Dunhill Cup (St. Andrews event)
19 Like much of Jesper Parnevik's clothing
20 Works in the pro shop
22 Toyota offering
25 "___ about time!"
26 Topped ball's movement
29 Australian golfer ___ Scott
30 Greens, essentially
33 It's opened by a sauna
34 Caddie, often
35 Justin Leonard, at the 1999 Ryder Cup
36 Caribbean island with a golf course designed by Robert Trent Jones II

37 2000 PGA Tour leader in sand saves, with 67% saved
41 Ponte Vedra ___
43 You can do it if your ball goes into the water
44 One more than bi-
47 Home of a PGA Tour
48 "That ___ his best swing" (golf announcer's line)
50 Continue
51 Cart path material
52 You might get one playing a few rounds in Hawaii
53 Jane or Bridget
54 NFL quarterback Jon
56 Foursome member, often
57 Apron of the green

60 2000 PGA Tour leader in driving accuracy, with 79.7% of fairways hit
65 ___ grand slam
66 It keeps the gallery back
67 "Understand?"
68 Shout "get in the hole!" from the stands
69 Loses a bet
70 Messy place

DOWN

1 "Amazing" or "spectacular": Abbr.
2 Heifer's statement
3 Derisive shout
4 Geezer
5 ___ Hole (St. Andrews stumper)
6 Tool that makes holes in leather

7 Many PGA tournaments last four
8 Cuts down, as a tree
9 Cartoon dog sounds
10 Gen ___
11 ___-iron
12 "The Simpsons" character Flanders
15 Makes better-tasting, perhaps
17 "Cheers" cry
21 "Ich bin ___ Berliner"
22 Truck part
23 "Without further ___ ..."
24 Billy who won twice on the 1998 Tour
26 "We have a problem" city
27 Outer space sphere

28 It annoyed the princess
30 Topped the field
31 Lofty shot's trajectory
32 See 52-Down
33 ___-tournament favorite
35 Nervous bit of laughter
36 Matterhorn or Jungfrau
38 Big name in electronics
39 It holds a lot of coffee
40 Poker stakes
41 Step up to the plate
42 That: Spanish
45 Lightning attractor
46 Once ___ lifetime
48 ___ hazard
49 LPGA player Leigh ___ Mills
50 "___ is deceptively simple": Arnold Palmer
52 With 32-Down, 2000 PGA Tour leader in all other major categories, including all-around
53 Doesn't hook
54 Patella's place
55 Big do
56 Mr. Le Pew
57 TV overseers
58 Cheerleader's cry
59 Extreme anger
61 Ticket info
62 Letters on ships
63 After expenses
64 Golf cart starter

ANSWER, PAGE 94

MM NUMBERS, PART 2

Now, from the ladies' tees.

ACROSS

1 Doesn't use one's own set of clubs
6 Skirt line
9 Be really shocking
14 Change one's game to suit course conditions
15 Down Under bird
16 Heat's city
17 2000 LPGA Tour leader in driving accuracy, with 86.3% of fairways hit
20 Dallas school where Payne Stewart went
21 He takes the stump
22 ___ out a win
23 "Thanks ___!"
25 Place for some cats
27 2000 LPGA Tour Rookie of the Year

34 Walks around sulking
35 Put on TV
36 Used to be
37 Unwelcome picnicker
38 "If Tomorrow Comes" author Sidney
42 Golfs, Jettas, etc.
43 Working hard
45 Actor Wallach
46 "___ the loneliest number ..."
48 2000 LPGA Tour leader in eagles (13), tied with Sophie Gustafson
52 New Year's ___
53 Kick out of office
54 Grind ___ halt
57 "___ the money ..."
60 ___ bunker (stuck)

63 2000 LPGA Tour leader in four categories, including all-around
67 ___ a putt short
68 ___-tournament favorite
69 Please, to Langer
70 Tom and family
71 Actor Beatty
72 Sing like Tormé

DOWN

1 Also-___ (losers)
2 Dutch cheese that comes in wax
3 Mork's sign-off
4 ___ at Sugarloaf
5 Place for piggies
6 Fireplace base
7 Jane Austen classic
8 Doesn't have a choice

9 Unable to tell right from wrong
10 Deep hole
11 Jerry of the Tour
12 One way to run
13 Citrus choice
18 Cheer for Tiger, maybe
19 1984 Bo Derek movie
23 Exist
24 Playoff disappointment
26 Puppy's offering
27 "___ know it!"
28 Vision-related
29 George Bush or George W. Bush
30 "What ___ I do wrong?" (question to the club pro)
31 Iron choice
32 U.S. Open winner, 1974, 1979, and 1990
33 Lawman Eliot

34 Address to a lady
39 Montana's capital
40 Letter after kay
41 Christmas drinks
44 In ___ rough
47 ___ King Cole
49 Brings out, as a feeling
50 With an anchor in the water
51 Find a fix
54 It's rude to do while another player is putting
55 "The ___ Love"
56 Biology subj.
58 Network that frequently airs golf tournaments
59 Warning from a driver
60 "Leave ___ me!"
61 Cold War side
62 Church cry
64 "___ had it!" (golfer's lament?)
65 "Today" letters
66 Title for British golfer Henry Cotton

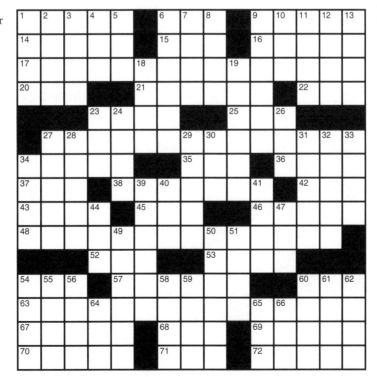

72ND IN '75

Reliving one of the great Masters.

ACROSS

1 Suffix often attached to Tiger's achievements
4 Emotionally damage
8 Big name in Masters history
13 ___ Lomond (Scottish course designed by 38-Across)
15 British PGA European Tour player Barry ___
16 PGA Tour schedule item
17 Atahualpa, notably
18 "M*A*S*H" star
19 On the tee
20 He missed his 15-foot putt on the final hole of the 1975 Masters, finishing one stroke behind the winner
23 "You ___ lucky!" (complaint to a playing partner)
24 Golf teacher, to some kids
25 Shade
28 ___ Solo (Harrison Ford role)
29 Cry to a ball that's thinking of rolling into the water
33 Play through

35 City that's home to the Schloss Schonborn Golf Club
37 Screams heard in bullrings
38 He missed his 8-foot putt on the final hole of the 1975 Masters, finishing one stroke behind the winner
41 Full of tension
43 Gallery noise that may distract a putter
44 ___ eagle
47 Sicily's famous volcano
48 Part of RSVP
51 Autograph-seeker's need
52 Bronx attraction
54 Place for Sunday driving?

56 He watched as both 20-Across and 38-Across missed their putts, which gave him the green jacket by one stroke
60 1969 LPGA leading money winner ___ Mann
63 Beem of the Tour
64 Periods in the past
65 Emerge as a contender
66 Herb used in creams
67 Sarazen who scored an albatross on his way to winning the 1935 Masters
68 She loved Jason
69 Fired, as a golf ball into the woods
70 Forsman of the Tour

DOWN

1 "Deep Impact" star Wood
2 Mexican state south of Arizona
3 He scored an albatross in the 1985 U.S. Open
4 Do in a dragon
5 Good way to be while putting
6 "The King ___"
7 King's territory
8 Irons employed in Hollywood
9 Word golfers don't like in their scores
10 Teachers' org.
11 Put a stop to
12 Home for future ham
14 ___ Christian Andersen
21 Queen song "___ Here"
22 ___ wedge

25 ___-swing
26 Put into action
27 Curvy letter
30 Cut, as a tree
31 Binary digits
32 "He's gonna use ___-iron for this one ..." (golf commentator's line)
34 John Paul II, e.g.
35 Head to the polls
36 "I hate to break up ___"
38 Go bad
39 1964 U.S. Open champ Venturi
40 Arkansas mountain
41 Recipe amt.
42 Uncouth sort
45 Shrub associated with Augusta National
46 White dwarf
48 Caught
49 Lizard with a long tail
50 Reduce in number
53 Veggies you might enjoy at the Masters
55 "Break ___!"
56 First name of the 1994 and 1999 Masters champ
57 Cleopatra's river
58 Windows feature
59 Country music legend Atkins
60 Twin-___ engine
61 Form of "to be"
62 Get ___ of (throw out)

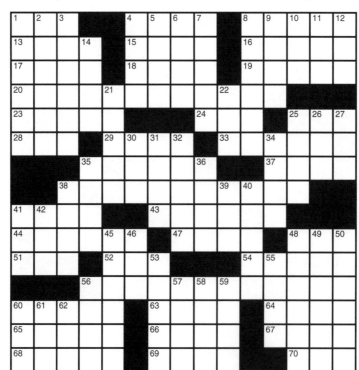

ANSWER, PAGE 80

A TRADITIONAL EDUCATION

Well, whaddya know?

ACROSS

1 Off in the distance, like a green
5 Card game similar to bridge
10 A-___ (Tiger often has it)
14 Flagstick
15 Quiet type of watercraft
16 October birthstone
17 City where The Countrywide Tradition takes place
19 St. Andrews's caddies, often
20 Refrain of a popular children's song
21 "___ Love Her"
22 Bogey-___ round
23 South African golf star
25 Head-shaking replies
27 Tom Kite, vis-à-vis The Countrywide Tradition in 2001
35 Title for many LPGA players
36 Rich cake
37 Scorecard box
38 Weekend Warriors' gp.
40 "I can't ___ only one here who ..."
42 ""¿Qué ___?" (Olazabal's greeting)

43 Navratilova rival
45 The body's biggest artery
47 Vucinich of the Senior PGA Tour
48 Club that hosts The Countrywide Tradition
51 Actress Peeples
52 It merged with Time Warner
53 Tom Wargo's real first name
56 "Sleepless in Seattle" actress
60 Highbrow entertainment
64 Clean off one's ball
65 He came in second at the first two Countrywide Traditions, but never won
67 Ms. Fitzgerald

68 Beethoven's "Für ___"
69 Dollar hundredth
70 Like some greens
71 Home on the plains
72 Arrives at one's score

DOWN

1 Church section with a domed roof
2 Fixed points, in geometry
3 Fleshy herb used for treating burns
4 Goosen of the Tour
5 Bathrooms, in Europe
6 ___ tough shot (faced a challenge on the course)

7 ___ instant (right away)
8 Convinced
9 ___ up
10 Where to buy accessories for your game
11 "And he taps in for ___" (golf announcer's line)
12 Converted, as a putt
13 "What ___ is new?"
18 For rent
24 Someone too good for your foursome
26 Nov. preceder
27 Aimed for the center of the fairway, maybe
28 Bob of the Tour
29 Hope to be the next Tiger Woods, perhaps

30 "Don't hit ___ hard" (advice from the club pro)
31 India's first prime minister
32 "Space Invaders" company
33 He may build a wall
34 Hit the links
35 TV's talking horse
39 1984 and 1995 Masters champ
41 Sicilian rumbler
44 Less than tetra-
46 Use as ___ (dig with one's sand wedge, maybe)
49 Where you're aiming the ball
50 South American beast prized for its wool
53 Knocks the gallery's socks off
54 Where a 10-Down might be located
55 Norway's ___ Golf Club
57 Ivy League golf team
58 "You've got ___ in your pants" (embarrassing thing to be told on the links)
59 NASDAQ rival
61 Looked over
62 Tear apart
63 They may be fine
66 ___ Wee Reese

FIRST THINGS FIRST

Don't give it a second thought.

ACROSS

1 Mr. Quigley
5 Take ___ practice swings
9 Catch the edge ___ bunker (nip the sand)
12 Worse than par
13 Bizarre art movement
14 Shout "fore!"
16 He won the 1st British Open
20 Lennon's partner on "Double Fantasy"
21 Callaway's Big ___ Driver
22 R-V links
23 Pod item
24 Small chicken
27 Bob Charles became the 1st one in 1963
33 General vicinities
34 Do some shoe work
35 ___ off (not even close, as a putt)
36 Had the impression of
37 Language suffix
40 Sharp sword
42 ___ Houston Open
44 He became the 1st European Masters champ in 1980
48 Tax ___
49 Putts ___ hole (PGA stat)
50 Oahu wear
51 Improve one's lie with one's shoe, e.g.
55 Place to get fit
58 1st woman to shoot a 59 in an LPGA event
62 Actress Garr
63 Baseball star on the Yankees, for short
64 Like two-foot putts
65 Big name in golf equipment

66 Loch ___ Monster
67 Liberal ___

DOWN

1 Inflict upon
2 Shakespeare's river
3 Captain in "20,000 Leagues Under the Sea"
4 Swing maker
5 "I have ___ ..."
6 "M*A*S*H" star who's a great friend of golf
7 Look over the story
8 Clean one's ball
9 Lose the bet
10 Bleacher creature
11 Huge record label
15 "I'm ___ I?" (pessimistic follow-up to "Am I on the green?")
17 Is silent when the marshal asks for silence, e.g.
18 Buffalo's hockey team
19 Meat cut
23 School gp.
25 Par three achievement
26 PGA : golf :: ___ : hockey
27 Murphy's ___ (it's often proven on the links)
28 Period of time
29 Oddly whimsical
30 Thin as ___
31 Ruby or diamond
32 Chicago airport
36 Ancient enemy of Athens
37 Suffix with mountain
38 ___-mo camera

39 Golf star who lives in the Bahamas
40 Color of some tees
41 Early English golfer Mitchell
42 Not in the mood for fooling around
43 That lady's
44 Actress Ward
45 Tour tournament
46 More high on oneself
47 Putting concerns
52 Strong ___ ox
53 "Encore!"
54 Tour players
55 Woods, Duval, or Mickelson
56 ___ champions (previous winners)
57 Alcott and Fruhwirth
59 George Gershwin's brother
60 Korean star Mi Hyun ___
61 View from Pebble Beach

ANSWER, PAGE 84

THIS PLACE IS A ZOO!

Animals spotted on the course.

ACROSS

1 Writer who coined the phrase "sour grapes"
6 Way short, as a putt
10 He yanked the 1986 PGA Championship away from Greg Norman by holing a bunker shot on the final hole
14 "The bombs bursting ___ ..."
15 Island: Spanish
16 Great putter from Japan
17 #2 or #13 at Augusta, for example
19 How you hold the club
20 Solid ___ rock
21 Herron of the Tour
22 Electric current unit
24 They help players with injuries: Abbr.
25 Polio vaccine inventor Salk
27 Player at Dubai
29 19th hole enjoyers, maybe
32 Warm capital
36 Suspect's defense

37 Where to keep score
38 Comedian's visual
39 Job for a jazzman
40 U.S. ___ Championship
43 Eighth planet from the sun: Abbr.
44 Weird look
46 "Render ___ Caesar ..."
47 "Who ___ kidding?"
49 Person who's signed up
51 Grabbed, as a title
52 Golf sweater material, maybe
53 Powerful chess pieces
55 Early golfing champ Diegel
57 "Loosen up a little ___" (advice from the club pro)

59 551
60 Prefix with natal
63 5-___
65 Prominent nickname in golf
68 Drained, as a putt
69 End in ___ (require a playoff)
70 ___ score
71 Caddie, for example: Abbr.
72 ___-do-well
73 ___ Domingo, Dominican Republic

DOWN

1 Verdi opera
2 "Dukes of Hazzard" character
3 Long, dramatic tale
4 Peanut ___

5 Capital city for Gary Player
6 She completes Fred's couple
7 Ending for Taiwan
8 Automaker ___-Romeo
9 Nepal's capital
10 Playground game
11 Topped ball, in slang
12 Just ___ (too young to do anything impressive, supposedly)
13 Green nerves
18 Cotton ___
23 ___ shop
25 Dubya's brother
26 Obliterate, as a course record
28 Swiss peak
29 Two-under result

30 Visitor from far, far away
31 His real first name is Eldrick
33 Big name in the cookie business
34 Lerner and ___ musicals
35 ___ the ante (started playing tougher)
37 Walking help
41 Discreetly taken freebie
42 31-Down often tops them
45 Aussie marsupial, for short
48 College dormitory workers: Abbr.
50 ___ wedge
51 ___ possession of the lead
54 More out there
55 Kind of bean
56 Past periods
58 Carry, as a bag of golf clubs
60 Gas associated with Vegas
61 Compass word
62 About
64 Driving range border
66 It may be surreptitiously improved with one's shoe
67 Bikini half

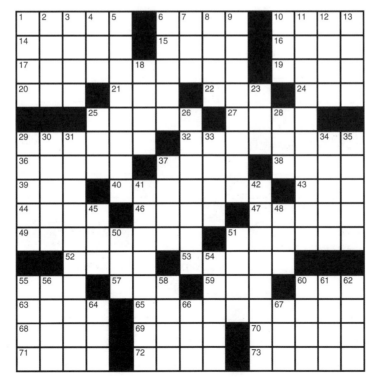

ANSWER, PAGE 86

19

THAT'S MY LPGA EVENT!

Name that tournament.

ACROSS

1 Not pro
5 First golf teacher, often
9 Tiger often takes off the week before one
14 Korean and Vietnam
15 "Let's just leave ___ that"
16 "Three Times ___"
17 The Office Depot hosted by ___
19 San ___, California
20 Won back, as the lead
21 Drain (a putt)
23 Wrath
24 This: Spanish
25 Where Billy Mayfair was a four-time All-American
27 Jones of the LPGA Tour
29 Say
31 Lions, Bears, etc.
33 Gets up and down, maybe
38 Line up off-target
41 "So what ___?"
42 Faced, as a shot
44 He caught Larsen's World Series perfect game
45 Hang overhead, as a branch
47 Tropical sight
49 Big name in electronics
50 Jamaican, maybe
52 Topping a ball or leaving a putt short
54 Conference David Duval was in when he played at Ga. Tech
56 Tooth-doctor's org.
59 Quiche ingredient
61 PDQ
63 Peter Jacobsen's home state
65 You shouldn't do it as you're putting
67 First Union ___ Classic
69 Show to be false
70 "___ in the water?" (question to a caddie)
71 General Robt. ___
72 Hawks
73 "___ back!" (cry to an overhit ball)
74 Letter start

DOWN

1 On top of things
2 "Vijay Singh" and "Phil Mickelson"
3 "___ hit it a little softer" (advice during a lesson)
4 Mr. Aoki
5 Concedes the hole
6 From ___ Z
7 Bradley and McGowan
8 Golf sweaters, e.g.
9 Green indentations
10 Pie ___ mode
11 ___ Kroger Classic
12 Golf shoes may have one after a day on the links
13 1984 National League MVP Sandberg
18 Mauna ___, Hawaii
22 Standard
26 State where you can play at the Park City Golf Course
28 Map-within-a-map
30 Bunkers
32 Money in Milan
33 Comedian Caesar
34 On the horizon
35 Electrolux USA Championship hosted by ___ and Amy Grant
36 J. Douglas ___, player Tommy Armour called "the best golfer I ever saw," who died mysteriously in Atlanta in 1921
37 The sun
39 Compaq rival
40 West of the silver screen
43 Golf stats, for example
46 God for lovers
48 Catherine ___, who won the 1967 U.S. Women's Open as an amateur
51 Language of Lebanon
53 Bunker tools
55 React to a bad round, maybe
56 Quick on one's feet
57 "I've ___ bad thing!"
58 Emotion felt after hooking a ball into the pond
59 Some tides
60 Extreme joy
62 Moolah in Mexico
64 ___ out a win
66 Zero, in soccer
68 Actor Robbins

ANSWER, PAGE 88

THE AYES HAVE IT

Look for two in a row.

ACROSS

1 "Pardon me," in Rome
6 Words on a prize at a county fair
11 Prefix with spin
14 Golfer with an army
15 "Your lights ___"
16 Modern medical gp.
17 Retief Goosen and Jim Estes list it as a hobby in their PGA Tour profiles
19 Will Smith's music style
20 Mix the ingredients
21 Inventor for whom the international unit of magnetic flux density is named
22 Roll call answer
23 Big name in mattresses
25 Hint for Sherlock
27 Considerate question on the green
33 LPGA great Bradley
36 Genesis hit "___ Deep"
37 Christmas bird
38 "Either it ___ it isn't!"
40 Perch atop the grass, as a golf ball
42 "I am ___ crook!"
43 Used a stopwatch
45 Locations
47 Homer Simpson outburst
48 PGA Tour event last held in 1998
51 Batman portrayer West
52 Holy type
55 Kansas ___
57 Lunn of the LPGA Tour
61 "And ___ goes"
63 Nincompoop
64 LPGA Hall of Famer who's done ads for Subaru
66 Warhol subject
67 "___ that note ..."
68 Cut the sentence up
69 Thousands of years
70 "The Second Coming" poet
71 Kind of attack

DOWN

1 Gets rid of a tree, maybe
2 Ending for bureau or pluto
3 Prepare to remove one's golf shoes
4 Club for environmentalists
5 Suffix with hotel or cloth
6 Rouse from slumber
7 Eye part
8 Young or Diamond
9 Tiny country where you can play at the Monte Carlo Golf Club
10 Tony Jacklin's nat.
11 Big club
12 Mr. Uresti
13 Vatican honcho
18 Golf shirt ruiners
22 One of five greats
24 Site of a Penna. nuclear accident
26 Carry around, as a set of golf clubs
28 "___ far, far better thing ...": Dickens
29 Away from home
30 "I want ___ do something for me ..."
31 Concerning
32 "Awesome!"
33 Essential part
34 Site of a PGA tour
35 Missouri-born star
39 Set to tee off
41 Stomach enzyme
44 Day, to Garcia
46 Black or Baltic
49 Guarded against
50 Altima maker
53 ___ Dame
54 ___ course record (has a great round, maybe)
55 ___ up short (just missed)
56 Mr. Aoki
58 "Manhattan Murder Mystery" star
59 Time to call in the National Guard
60 Disturbances
62 Odyssey
64 Tour player ___ Don Blake
65 Mess tent workers, for short

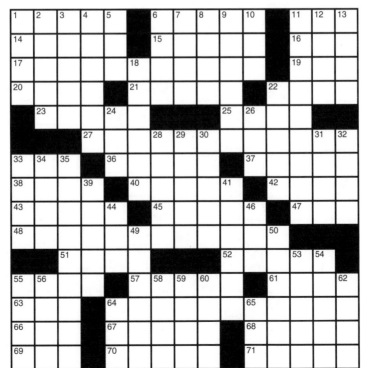

ANSWER, PAGE 90

TIGER CATCHING

Pros who've caught Tiger when he was leading after 54.

ACROSS

1 It's attached to a golf bag
6 Cries from the gallery
10 Opposite of "fore"—on a boat, that is
13 ___ look (peek)
14 Ending for switch
15 Russian space station that crashed to earth
16 He shot a 64 to overtake Tiger in the final round of the 2000 Deutsche Bank SAP Open
18 Monopoly property, often: Abbr.
19 ___ Jima
20 Section of New York or London
21 Golfing Clarke
23 Dict. entries
25 Santa ___, Calif.
27 "So ___!"
28 He shot a 67 to overtake Tiger in the final round of the 1996 Quad Cities Classic
31 Extremely skilled person
34 ___-mo camera
35 Dan of the Tour
36 A hundred score pounds
37 He shot a 66 to overtake Tiger in the final round of the 2000 Tour Championship
41 ___ Paulo, Brazil

42 Woosnam and Baker-Finch
43 No longer playing competitively: Abbr.
44 Like laying up, often
46 Gives to charity
50 "___ long par four ..." (golf announcer's line)
51 Shotmaking concern
53 Any U.S. Ryder Cup team player, to Brits
54 Recurring motifs
57 Org. that oversees many golf tournaments
60 Niihau neckwear
61 They take a chunk out of every American golfer's prize money

62 He shot a 69 to overtake Tiger in the final round of the 2001 Dubai Desert Classic
65 Powerful union: Abbr.
66 Inside of a golf ball
67 Casual forms of speech
68 "___ in the hole!"
69 Golf cart noise-maker
70 Full of current events

DOWN

1 Got madder and madder but didn't say anything
2 Get the round going
3 Like some talent

4 Clubhouse drinks, frequently
5 El ___
6 Victorious cry after a team match
7 Gold: Spanish
8 Willie of the Tour
9 Another clubhouse drink
10 Another clubhouse drink, if the bar is well-stocked
11 Mid-distance choice
12 New Jersey's capital
13 Take a tumble down the rankings
17 Popular cuisine
22 Tony Dorsett and Walter Payton, for two: Abbr.

24 Exultant shout from Sergio Garcia
26 Run ___ (go crazy)
29 North of politics
30 Popular style of architecture
32 "Don't be ___!"
33 Popular 1990s sitcom
35 Desk toppers, for short
37 Like many short holes
38 Watched the place while the owner was away
39 All over the world: Abbr.
40 "___ with us, we'll be right back" (golf announcer's line)
41 Acting maliciously
45 Hydroelectric power source
46 Prefix meaning "ten"
47 Eagle's claws
48 Get-up-and-go
49 Famed foursome event
52 "___ this blunder still you find": Hannah More
55 Create a certain kind of art
56 "Beat it, gnat!"
58 Part of PGA
59 Skilled
63 Gary of Scottish golf
64 A boxer's may get broken

ANSWER, PAGE 92

CORRECT, CORRECT, CORRECT!

A trivia question with three right answers.

ACROSS

1 The, to Langer
4 Brakes and slides
9 See 13-Down
14 Fall Classic mo.
15 Fable guy
16 German sub
17 Part 1 of trivia question
19 39.37 inches, in England
20 You can get it from PGATour.com
21 Chicken or chicken noodle
23 Transportation for rough riding: Abbr.
24 Part 2 of trivia question
29 "Where ___?"
32 Ryder Cup team: Abbr.
33 "And to say ___ more": Shakespeare
34 Part 3 of trivia question
37 Bunker
41 Works at the bar
42 Walker, on signs
44 1999 FedEx St. Jude Classic champ

45 Ungolfable weather
46 Correct answer #1
48 Sacred bird of the Nile
52 "We ___ the World"
53 Part of DOS
54 Correct answer #2
59 ___ loss for words
60 One of Donald Duck's nephews
61 Canyon noise
65 Energy
67 Correct answer #3
71 Country home to the oldest golf club outside the British Isles
72 Gangster Bugs
73 1959 Masters champ ___ Wall, Jr.
74 ___ out (beat by a stroke)
75 Standing upright

76 Aussie hopper, for short

DOWN

1 A few strokes behind
2 Aspirin fights it
3 Pack away
4 ___ Paulo, Brazil
5 1964 U.S. Open winner Venturi
6 Ending for final
7 Use a divining rod
8 Sundae utensils
9 Enter the conversation abruptly
10 UK title
11 ___ this time (maybe later)
12 Divot material
13 With 9-Across, 1996 U.S. Open winner
18 Northwestern sch.

22 ___ Tour (Bob Hope specialty)
25 Bunches of clubs
26 Avignon affirmation
27 ___ school (where some learn golf)
28 ___ Dame
29 Creatures you may find on your golf ball
30 Demeanor
31 ___ way (not at all)
35 ___ Watts golf shops
36 Date
38 Some hard liquors
39 With skill
40 Season ___ (public course buy)
43 Hard-to-master golf tactic
44 Part of a wedding cake

47 Second Amendment org.
49 Punish, French Revolution-style
50 Where Bird played college ball: Abbr.
51 Sailor's protector
54 1995 U.S. Open winner—with an even score
55 "Jack Sprat ___ fat"
56 Hole measurement
57 "Keep your ___ the ball!"
58 Number of Masters Tiger will win, according to a Nicklaus prediction
62 Basil or Nicholas
63 Greg Norman, to many Aussies
64 Not fooled by
66 Compete
68 Before, in poems
69 1983 U.S. Women's Open champ Stephenson
70 4 ___ 3 (match play result)

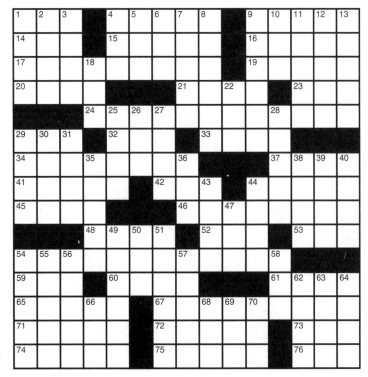

FROM THE CLUBHOUSE TO THE WHITE HOUSE

Golf tales from Washington.

ACROSS

1 President who, when told that a visiting head of state had arrived, announced "I'll be damned if I'll give up my game to see this fellow," and resumed his round of golf
5 ___ year (annually)
10 Uppercut target
13 Prefix meaning "high"
14 Moves like a putted ball
15 Kind of list
16 President whose father and grandfather both served as USGA president
18 It hosted three 2000 LPGA events
19 Double ___
20 Made, as money
22 Weaken
25 Tavern owner on "The Simpsons"
26 "Humanity does not ___ to be happy": Orson Scott Card
27 Like some golfers, or some golf balls
29 "Gentlemen Prefer Blondes" blonde
32 Evans and Carnegie
33 Flower associated with Holland

34 Lions, Bears, etc.
37 Emerald ___ (Ireland)
38 ___ St. Jude Classic
39 "The ___ Love"
40 Key on a computer
41 Makes one
42 Flour might go through it
43 How the gallery might react to a great shot
45 ___ Bear (golf moniker)
46 They're won in November
48 Oriole Ripken
49 Decade pts.
50 Marquee word
52 North of politics
54 "___ put it another way ..."

55 President coached by Jack Nicklaus, Hale Irwin, and Dave Stockton
60 Lowly laborer
61 Lodge a complaint
62 Like the hair of 16-Across and 24-Down
63 ___ Diego
64 Disrespectful
65 Bob who said, "I'd give up golf if I didn't have so many sweaters"

DOWN

1 Kids' game
2 Links highlight
3 To and ___
4 Ripped, as a scorecard after a bad round?

5 Washington neighbor
6 Worthy of esteem
7 Footprint or fingerprint
8 Johannesburg-born star
9 Late tennis great Arthur
10 Most skilled golfer among U.S. presidents
11 Goodbye, at the Evian Masters
12 Enjoyer of a major 15-stroke victory
15 Body's trunk
17 Golf and chess
21 Powerful D.C. lobby
22 Bauer who makes golf apparel

23 Some putter heads are made of it
24 President who owns 70 putters
28 Two letters after tee
29 Like some difficult golfing conditions
30 Cries of praise
31 Say no to
33 Report a playground infraction
35 Mania
36 They're sometimes put on houses
38 Gave some grub
39 Kuwait has a lot of it
41 ___-win situation
42 Not hollow
44 Tear evoker
45 Ship's kitchen
46 Comes to a halt
47 Pak's peninsula
48 Shows approval, like a fan might
51 Omelet components
52 "___ he on his horse?": Shakespeare, "Antony and Cleopatra"
53 D followers
56 NOW cause
57 Gold, to a conquistador
58 Chitchat
59 Make a white shirt green

ANSWER, PAGE 79

WHERE TO THIS YEAR, OLD CHAP?

Venues of the oldest major.

ACROSS

1 "This ___ the greatest championship I have known" (Sarazen's evaluation of Greg Norman's 1993 British Open win)
4 "Do you ___?" (Carnoustie lost ball searcher's question?)
9 Five-time British Open winner Thomson
14 Here, to Henri
15 1960 British Open winner Kel
16 In for ___ awakening
17 Site of Norman's 1993 Open win
19 Like British Open crowds
20 Orlando, to Tiger
21 Site of two of Seve's three British Open victories
23 Actor Beatty
24 Three-time British Open champ
26 Belgrade resident
28 Tee ___
30 Most agile
33 Home to Jumbo Ozaki
37 Number of times Ben Hogan won the British Open
39 Shot for a dogleg, maybe
40 Light tan shade
41 Site of Open victories by Weiskopf, Watson, and Calcavecchia
42 Ending meaning "place of business"
43 Took to the hills
44 Work at a magazine
45 Good way to make a witty comment
46 Combinations
48 Anat., for example
50 Playground players
51 Garden surrounder
55 Plant seeds
57 "Do you ___?"
61 "___ Need Is a Miracle"
63 1994 British Open champ
65 Site of Trevino's classic 1972 Open victory over Nicklaus and Jacklin
67 Happen
68 Stan's partner
69 0
70 Wins, as a championship
71 Graf rival
72 Compass dir.

DOWN

1 Hope and pray
2 ___ God (uncontrollable event)
3 18th Greek letter
4 ___-cone
5 ___ Liverpool (former British prime minister)
6 Like good flan
7 Belinda Carlisle song "Should ___ You In?"
8 Former "Entertainment Tonight" host John
9 '60s winner of back-to-back British Opens
10 Time period
11 Site of Greg Norman's 1986 Open win
12 Green's border
13 Clarinetist's mouthpiece
18 Fish eaten as a delicacy in Spain
22 Colorado resort
25 January in golf
27 America's Cup, sometimes?
29 Two-time major winner Doug and family
30 British Open hosts, often
31 Go too far, as an approach shot
32 1986 PGA Championship winner
33 1988 PGA Championship winner Sluman
34 Rights-focused org.
35 Site of the first 12 British Opens
36 Video's counterpart
38 "___ didn't!" (denier's phrase)
41 Like final-round atmosphere
45 Six-sided roller
47 The rest
49 Tony Blair's wife
52 ___ Rees (greatest British player never to win a British Open, some would say)
53 Day and others
54 Island of New York
55 Dalmatian feature
56 Killer whale of movie fame
58 "Famous" cookie maker
59 Breaking it might cost you strokes
60 Where flour is ground
62 Doing nothing
64 Pool stick
66 Moroccan city with a hat named after it

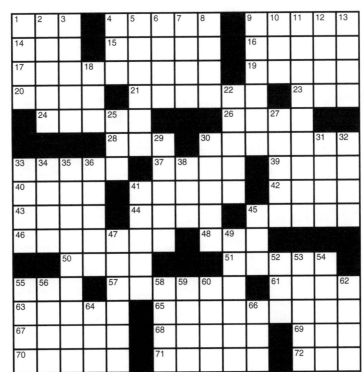

ANSWER, PAGE 80

25

MADE IN THE SHADE

Some of golf's colorful characters.

ACROSS

1 Camera name
6 Schoolkid's helper
11 Marc or Wayne, to Gary Player
14 More than like
15 Sphere of battle
16 Popular card game
17 Three-time top-10 finisher on the 1999 Tour
19 ___ for tat
20 Gets better, in a way
21 Haul before a judge
22 Kite or Scherrer
23 The ___ crust
26 Spot
27 In the ___ (playing well)
28 Piece of golf apparel
29 Knox and Bragg: Abbr.
30 Crenshaw and Hogan
31 Give a bad review to
32 Twosome
34 Lob wedge shots get a lot of it
35 Tiger Woods edged him out at the 1999 Buick Invitational

40 "I threw away my golf shoes when I got a hole-in-one," for example
41 Demand
42 Stroke, as a golf ball
44 Cabin components
46 ___ Tour
47 "Citizen ___"
48 Baby's first word, maybe
49 ___ time
50 Lessened
52 Have debts outstanding
53 Corn's home
54 Phone co. worker
55 Nest egg letters
56 Winner of the 2000 Audi Senior Open
61 Address for Paul McCartney

62 Religion of over a billion
63 Airplane's middle
64 British Open meal
65 Senior PGA Tour pro who took up golf at age 23
66 Beatles tune "___ Is"

DOWN

1 Saturn or Mercury
2 Bother
3 "Smoking or ___?"
4 Highly decorative
5 Horse's sound
6 Keep ___ on (watch)
7 www.pgatour.com, for instance
8 Heckles
9 As scheduled
10 Trap tool
11 Hal on the links
12 They'll make you cry
13 Denier's phrase
18 Ending for employ or honor
23 Weird claim
24 Captain of "Moby Dick"
25 Rice-a-___
26 Last player to win back-to-back U.S. Opens
27 Number of British Opens Fuzzy Zoeller won
29 Kind of pine
30 It should watch out for nine-iron shots
32 Word in many Carnoustie scores
33 Novelist Rand

34 Early 1900's British great ___ Mitchell
36 Org. for Mallon
37 House of Representatives vote
38 Cry of surprise
39 Front or back, in golf
43 Ray or Tryba
44 He snatched a major from Van De Velde
45 1998 is probably his favorite year
46 ___ Beach
47 One of Annika's rivals
48 Like good cake
49 "He's going ___ a five-iron here ..." (announcer's phrase)
50 Likely
51 Noted Navajo golfer
53 It might be holed
54 "It's either him ___!"
57 Enjoy the nineteenth hole, maybe
58 Curvy letter
59 Inventor Whitney
60 Driving range feature

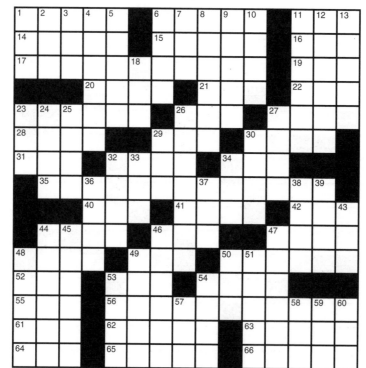

ANSWER, PAGE 82

NIZHONI!

Learn more about a Notah-ble golfer.

ACROSS

1 Headache stopper
6 Clubhouse utensil
10 "I didn't take a single mulligan today," maybe
13 Hotel offering
14 Three-time U.S. Women's Open champ ___ Maxwell Berning
15 Beatles tune "___ Loser"
16 ___ Classic (one of Notah Begay's Tour wins)
18 Hefty
19 "Up and ___!"
20 Neckwear in Hawaii
21 The "up" in "get up and down"
23 Australian jumper, for short
24 Like good golf scores
25 Poor
27 "Kablooey!"
28 Scottish star Sam
31 J.L. on the PGA Tour
34 Stockton or Marr
35 Notah Ryan Begay ___
36 Chick who won the U.S. Open and U.S. Amateur in the same year (1916)
37 ___ tree (cornered)
38 "___ the Barbarian"
40 Golf instructor ___ Sole
41 Blvds.
42 Popular cookies
43 Fayetteville's state
46 Eighteen-wheeler
47 Computer letters
48 Tournament attendee
49 Three or four, often
52 Fifth episode of a miniseries
54 Lousy newspaper
55 Magazine that in 1997 named Tiger Woods one of the 25 most influential people in America
56 Wedge shot's path
57 Notah's birthplace and home
61 Payne Stewart's alma mater
62 Not exactly proper golfing attire
63 He created the Lorax
64 Recipe measurement: Abbr.
65 They might be stacked against you
66 He won nine PGA Tour events between 1982 and 1985

DOWN

1 ___ as the eye can see
2 Because of
3 Instructional ___ (golfer's purchase)
4 Catalog entry
5 Evil Luthor
6 Mountain visible from the Taiheiyo Club's Gotemba golf course
7 Big Midwestern sch.
8 Free (of)
9 Greens ending
10 Notah was the first Buy.com Tour golfer to shoot this score in a tournament
11 Apple product
12 Rubber ducky's milieu
14 Gumbo or goulash
17 Like some foursomes
22 Mont. neighbor
24 Ryder Cup letdown
25 Sky wonders
26 Prior to
27 ___ placement (golfer's concern)
28 Gets on film
29 Hollywood "bye!"
30 One in Oberbayern
31 1964 British Open champ Tony
32 At any time
33 Notah played on this U.S. team in 1995
34 Mickelson rival
38 It's tossed
39 Assn.
41 "___ told you before ..."
44 Total: Abbr.
45 Notah's ancestral language, in which this puzzle's title means "Nicely done!"
46 Spaghetti sauce brand
48 Website info sections, for short
49 Arouse, as interest
50 In ___-win situation
51 Piece maker?
52 Yesteryear
53 Golf swing performers
54 Travels, as a putt
55 Natural course hazard
58 Was winning the tournament
59 Like some lies, in golf
60 Sixth sense letters

CADDYSHACK

Featuring some super loopers.

ACROSS

1 Golf course headgear
5 Alter kitty
9 He won four majors in the '90s
14 "There oughta be ___ against that!"
15 Grow weary, as on the back nine
16 Make, as a putt
17 Payne Stewart's longtime caddie, whom he hugged famously after winning the 1999 U.S. Open
19 Get ___ awakening
20 Finnish entree
21 "___ that wrong?"
22 Tiger's former caddie, often described as a "Deadhead"
30 "Give it ___!"
31 Full of holes
32 Covered, as with gold
33 You have to do it if you didn't bring your own clubs
34 Guy's counterpart
37 British ___ (golf's birthplace)
39 H.S. diploma alternative
40 Kind of camera used for sporting events
42 Half a famous golf name
43 Olympic skating champ Lipinski
45 Heading, as the leader board
46 Restaurant patrons
48 "___ you!" ("Go ahead, make my day!")
49 Veteran caddie who has worked for Tom Lehman
52 Lose, as a lead
53 Site: Abbr.
54 Sorenstam, to Webb
56 David Duval's longtime caddie
62 Woman who won the U.S. Open six times—but not in golf
63 "Hold on ___!"
64 Feminine ending
65 Works with a blowtorch
66 Fool
67 In the vicinity

DOWN

1 Twin-___ engine
2 Big name in boxing
3 Three-time winner on the 1999 Ladies' Tour
4 Gabriel Hjertstedt's nat.
5 How to stand when someone else is putting
6 Gain, as strokes
7 Biblical boat
8 "I made the putt!"
9 Agcy. that approves medicines
10 Robin Hood's weapons
11 Driving Miss Davies
12 Offed
13 Mind ___ manners
18 Quality of John Daly or Craig Stadler
22 Tiger's play, to some
23 Like Darren Clarke
24 Big first name on the Ladies' Tour
25 East, to Olazabal
26 It might shake if you get the yips
27 Funk on the links
28 Prisoner
29 Pop flies, usually
34 ___ unlucky bounce (had some golf misfortune)
35 Dean Martin tune "That's ___"
36 LPGA Hall of famer
38 Mickelson or Sutton
39 Expanded
41 ___-da (pretentious)
44 Had
46 Fiori, formally
47 Like some peanuts
48 Putting distraction
49 Still in the hunt for first place
50 Unheard of
51 Mediate on the golf course
52 Clubhouse drink
55 Sgt. superiors
56 Throwing golf clubs, kicking the sand trap, etc.
57 Prefix that means "similar"
58 1964 U.S. Open winner Venturi
59 Compass dir.
60 ___ hot streak
61 Gen ___ (25–34 year old, approximately)

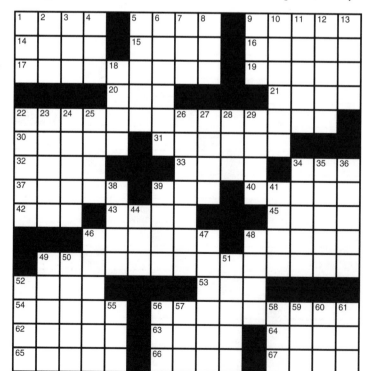

THAT'S WHAT THEY CALL ME

Golf nicknames.

ACROSS

1 See 45-Across
6 Pronoun for Pak
9 He won three majors in 1953
14 Cod and Hatteras
15 "Psst!"
16 "... in Order to form ___ perfect Union ..."
17 Sarazen
19 ___ whopper (lie)
20 Weather ___
21 Before, in combinations
22 Tailor, often
23 Palmer
26 Em followers
27 Golf pro's offering
30 Constellation with a belt
33 Cotton gin inventor Whitney
34 Aleve rival
37 Worthy of praise
40 More skilled
42 Ore-___ french fries
43 Impudence, to the British
44 Toms or Graham
45 With 1-Across, noted celebrity golf patron
47 Had a hoagie
48 Come after
50 "Heart of Darkness" author Joseph
52 Putting ___ par
54 (Steve) Pate
57 Home to the Moscow City Golf Club
60 Crew team's equipment
61 Disrupt a player on the tee, maybe
65 Like King Atahualpa
66 Nelson
68 ___ Lodge
69 ___ for (choose, as a club size)
70 Paris's river
71 Put off
72 Long-eared animal
73 Performer's spot

DOWN

1 Erstwhile comedy show based in Chicago
2 Laugher's sound
3 B.C. ___
4 Starts over
5 Lawyer's letters
6 Fail to be a model employee
7 "___ go again!"
8 CBS logo
9 More than dislike
10 Sign of the future
11 Nicklaus
12 Politician Specter
13 Gets close
18 Topple
22 Mark McCormack, notably: Abbr.
24 Doesn't share
25 PGA Tour player Henke
27 Stroke advantage
28 Island where Napoleon was exiled
29 Armour
31 Korean port where MacArthur landed
32 Reaction to missing a gimme
35 Picture portion of a telecast
36 Former dictator Amin
38 "Don't ___ silly little thing like that bother you!"
39 ___ out a victory (just barely won)
41 German "a"
46 "Pick ___" (magician's instruction)
49 Sch. founded by Jefferson
51 Soon
52 Like some clubhouse food
53 Pound sixteenth
55 Caddies (for)
56 Golf course vehicles
58 Not nuts
59 "Are you ___ out?"
62 Song from an opera
63 Like some par fours
64 Big joint
66 Mauna ___, Hawaii
67 Many college degs.

ANSWER, PAGE 88

HOLE OF HORRORS

We've all had this experience.

ACROSS

1 Actor Estrada
5 Snap, as a winless streak
8 You have to read it when putting
13 See 25-Across
15 Aussie animal
16 The body's largest artery
17 Legend automaker
18 Chemical suffix
19 Out of practice
20 "First, I managed to ___ all of thirty yards."
23 Prefix with metric
24 Woosnam or Baker-Finch
25 With 13-Across, when golfers start their rounds
28 "My next shot looked OK until it hooked and ___."
34 Actress Gardner
35 Layer, as of a wedding cake
36 "___ Frutti"
37 Tape made by a band
39 Chocolate substitute
42 Section
43 Power tool
45 "As I was going to St. ___ ..."
47 Diegel or DiCaprio
48 "After I took a penalty, my approach shot ___."
52 Home to Tony Jacklin: Abbr.
53 Lean-___ (building adjuncts)
54 Letters in a classified ad
55 "And to top it all off, after pitching out ___. And there were still 17 holes to play ..."

61 John on the farm
64 Geiberger and others
65 ___ Janeiro
66 Using the wrong size club, e.g.
67 Sixth sense
68 Carried
69 Doesn't stand up straight
70 Mattiace of the Tour
71 Close at hand

DOWN

1 Coup d'___
2 Puerto ___
3 Words from a golfer who's next in line to drive
4 Zarley of the Senior PGA Tour
5 One of the Great Lakes
6 Zero
7 "Easy ___!"
8 Member of the nobility
9 Easy Ryder Cup win
10 Hosp. places
11 Sponsor of a Pebble Beach tournament
12 Letter after jay
14 Captures a thought perfectly
21 Gin and ___
22 "Yeah, right!"
25 "I've got ___ to you!"
26 Main dish
27 "Golfweek" worker
28 Walk like a duck
29 "Thou wast ___ obstinate heretic": Shakespeare, "Much Ado About Nothing"

30 Choosing as a member of, as a team
31 Lipton product
32 Senator Hatch
33 Little dog
38 ___ Tom Morris (golf legend)
40 Eggs, in biology
41 Jazz offshoot
44 Fans write them to Tiger
46 Golf course location, perhaps
49 Cry from Homer Simpson
50 Country where you can play a round at Caesarea
51 Idea
55 Golf bag object
56 "What ___ is new?"
57 Cable staple
58 Ripped
59 Novelist Ferber
60 Golf course visitor, often
61 State on the Atl.
62 Preceding
63 Pitching stat

ANSWER, PAGE 90

IN THE BEGINNING

A puzzle that takes you way back.

ACROSS

1 Canadian pro Dave
5 Rogers and Vucinich
9 Golf course admonitions
12 One of Gary's rivals
13 Company bigwigs
15 Skitter along, as an iron shot
16 Scotsman who banned golf in 1457 because it took time away from military training
18 ___ carte
19 "That's just the way ___!"
20 Golfer's summertime acquisition
21 Shoes for Tiger
23 S. ___ (Wyo. neighbor)
24 Brash boxer
25 Tiger's caddie
27 American city that outlawed golf from its streets in 1659, marking the sport's first official mention in the New World

32 Runner-up at the 2000 Masters, U.S. Open, and British Open
33 Lubricate
34 Greens ___
35 Make, as a putt
38 Stick's home
39 Like lob wedge shots
41 Masters mo.
42 Long, as a drive
43 Part of DOS
44 Golf's first trophy, awarded in Edinburgh in 1744
49 Golf patron Farr
50 Padraig Harrington's country: Abbr.
51 Boy at St. Andrews
54 Steam bath
56 One of the Gabor sisters

57 Military installation
58 ___ Tom Morris (second British Open winner)
59 Material from which golf balls were made starting in 1848
63 B.A. or B.S.
64 Swashbuckler Flynn
65 Did a sand trap chore
66 Cancel
67 Camera part
68 Part of PGA

DOWN

1 Water filter company
2 First name in Swedish golf
3 Fixes the outcome
4 Not accepted: Abbr.

5 Stay, as in the lead
6 Beasts of burden
7 "What can I do for you?"
8 ___-fi
9 Don't be annoyed by, as a bogey
10 Make a chip shot
11 Healthful vacation spots
12 "You're just ___!"
14 Tendon
17 Book for travelers
22 Harvard Yard vegetation
24 With skill
25 Make the cut?
26 ___ Aviv
28 Permit
29 "___ on the green" (welcome words on the links)
30 No longer playing: Abbr.

31 Golf cart starter
35 Enjoy gyros
36 Speed stat
37 Be closed-minded
38 Utterly collapse under pressure
39 1988 Masters winner
40 Columbus sch.
42 Golf suffix for Max
43 Little bit of food
45 ___ Quentin
46 Public persona
47 Hogan and Snead, e.g.
48 PGA Tour player Ronnie and family
52 Pale
53 Absolutely unplayable, as a shot stuck in gorse
54 Clubhouse drink
55 First name of 1906 U.S. Open winner Smith and 1907 U.S. Open winner Ross
56 Famed English prep school
57 Feminists burned theirs in the 1970s
60 Web address: Abbr.
61 Three, in Rome
62 Paleozoic ___

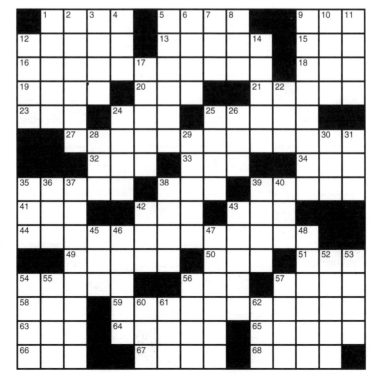

ANSWER, PAGE 92

PGA CHAMPIONSHIP TALE

An amazing story from the early days.

ACROSS

1 First name of 1998's PGA Championship winner
6 David who won twice on the 1999 PGA Tour
10 Englishman's exclamation of shock
14 Great Plains metropolis
15 "Four and twenty blackbirds baked in ___"
16 Prefix meaning "ten"
17 It's awarded to the winner of the PGA Championship
20 Main and Elm: Abbr.
21 PGA Tour players
22 Pre-deal money
23 Aid, as in crime
25 Somewhat
27 Golfer who in 1928, when the time came to relinquish the 17-Across, which he had won the year before, could not locate it
31 Noah's boat
34 Response to "Tiger won the tournament!," maybe
35 Sherlock Holmes and others: Abbr.
36 Elder or Janzen
37 Actor Diggs of "How Stella Got Her Groove Back"
38 Cut taxes
40 Move like a putt

41 Aussie bird that can't fly
42 On
43 Taj ___
44 George Bush or Dan Quayle: Abbr.
45 Where the 17-Across ended up, 27-Across believed
48 Ryder Cup team head: Abbr.
49 ___ in for par
50 Big piece of steel
53 Scottish golfer Gary
54 Chemical suffix
57 City where the 17-Across randomly turned up in a factory, two years later
62 Time before Easter
63 Front ___

64 "___ you so!"
65 Times
66 In the thick of
67 1963 U.S. Women's Open winner Mills and others

DOWN

1 They're taken at weddings
2 "___ the end of my rope!"
3 Stephenson and Brady
4 Shout of a person who's finally located a lost ball in the woods
5 Potato cousin
6 "The Lord ___ away" (Biblical line referring to Van De Velde's 1999 British Open experience?)

7 B.C. ___
8 Russian space station
9 Full array of golf clubs
10 "___ believe it!"
11 Fall mo.
12 It's a pain
13 Shouts of victory
18 Part of AARP
19 Stops play, perhaps
23 End in ___ (require a playoff)
24 Two-time Masters champ Crenshaw
25 Qualifies for the Senior PGA Tour?
26 Daniel of golf fame
27 ___ hazard (course worry)

28 Tiger's term for optimal performance
29 Play it cautiously
30 Change one's swing, say
31 Hawaiian hello
32 Advice to those with the yips
33 Ladies' star Kuehne
38 Part of a process
39 A driver won't give you much of it
40 Mild golf course utterance
42 Famed Texas building
43 Atlas page
46 Words from the narrowly defeated
47 Undercover cop of a sort
48 Links zoomers
50 Just hanging around
51 Michelob Championship drink
52 Sicily's famous volcano Mt. ___
53 Prefix with present
54 Dr. Frankenstein's assistant
55 Surprise winner of the 1991 PGA Championship
56 Puts a halt to
58 ___ slump (playing poorly)
59 1999 Bay Hill Invitational winner Herron
60 That guy
61 "Give ___ shot!"

ANSWER, PAGE 94

TRAGIC TRIVIA

About a man who's had major bad luck.

ACROSS

1 Lady's title
6 "Little Man ___" (1991 Jodie Foster movie)
10 Thirteen-time member of the Canadian World Cup team
14 Stick out like ___ thumb
15 "I cannot tell ___!"
16 See 26-Down
17 Part 1 of trivia question
19 Sounds from unruly fans
20 Network: Abbr.
21 A few strokes up
22 Come up ___ (lose)
23 Zillions
24 Lawyers' org.
25 Part 2 of trivia question
33 Have ___ sense of (be knowledgeable)
34 Surname of the 1947 and 1995 British Open winners
35 1979 Sally Field film "Norma ___"
36 States of anger
37 Assigns twosomes
39 Dreaded word to hear on the links
40 Talking-___ (admonitions)

41 Like Jan Stephenson or Phil Mickelson, many say
42 ___ in (clicked on the golf)
43 End of trivia question
47 "___ Wiedersehen!" (44-Down's goodbye)
48 Runner-up to Nicklaus at the 1980 U.S. Open
49 Backup strategy
52 Native American transport
54 Seal, as a victory
57 How a hole may play
58 Answer to trivia question
60 Tyler or Bancroft
61 Hardly worth mentioning

62 Spotted, as one's ball in the rough
63 PGA season, roughly
64 Some birdies
65 Tiger pumps his

DOWN

1 Paws' mates
2 Pallid
3 "___ I say!"
4 Swinging a golf club, to some
5 Nuclear bomb measurement
6 Coaches try to spot it in juniors
7 Automaker ___-Romeo
8 Like the 2000 PGA Championship, after 72 holes
9 Suffix with ballad
10 He ran with Tiger

11 "It's just ___, skip, and a jump away" (golfer's description of his ball's location after a mulligan?)
12 The National Guard might end it
13 Pinkish
18 Exclamations of discovery
22 Website where you can bid on golf equipment
23 Pints
24 First word of a Shakespeare title
25 French-speaking island nation
26 With 16-Across, rubber capital of the world
27 ___ problem with (predicts trouble)

28 Goodbye, in Grenoble
29 Course standard
30 University of Maine's town
31 Ending for sea or way
32 Makes friends with ducks
37 Dragon of song
38 From ___ Z (totally)
39 Sacred mountain of Japan
41 Lob wedge, say
42 Sit out, as a tournament
44 Two-time green jacket wearer
45 Good places to drive
46 Where Alan Shepard hit two golf balls with a six-iron, 2/6/71
49 Hit the links
50 ___ Star State (Texas)
51 "___ Karenina"
52 Grounds ___ (golf course employees)
53 Prefix meaning "flight"
54 Radio shock-jock Don
55 Lacks the power
56 Comes to a close
58 World standard clock setting: Abbr.
59 King, in 25-Down

YOU SAID A MOUTHFUL!

Some of golf's longer surnames.

ACROSS

1 Pro shop events
6 Talks endlessly about a birdie, say
11 Bit of putting advice, maybe
14 Really, really want
15 Extend the subscription
16 Go courting
17 1992 U.S. Solheim Cup team member
19 Personal
20 Mauna ___, Hawaii
21 Like many golfers after playing the Mercedes Championships
22 Tour man Tryba
23 10% of his player's winnings, for some caddies
24 Botches the job
26 They help you visit www.pgatour.com
28 Water, to Jean Van De Velde
30 Rachel of the LPGA
36 "___ your side!"
38 ___ Canada Championship
39 Sicily's Mt. ___
40 Appleby, casually
41 Understood
45 Title for Nero, Claudius, or Bobby Jones: Abbr.
46 Cuba or Dominica, in Spanish
48 Inventor Whitney
49 Take the cart
51 Mark on the green?
55 Ending with cloth or bombard
56 Mi Hyun ___
57 Political cartoonist Thomas
61 ___ John (Daly)
63 Boxing name
66 ___ and don'ts
68 Revolutionary Guevara
69 Michigan city
70 He called his final round 65 at the 1988 British Open the best 18 holes of his life
73 "___ jour!"
74 Lazy sort
75 Mark McCormack, notably
76 Three-time major bridesmaid of 2000
77 Donkeys and burros
78 Valentine's Day bouquet

DOWN

1 Dieter's tool
2 Knight's protection
3 Senator Alexander
4 LPGA Tour player Dahllof
5 Religious offshoot
6 If your practice swing hits one, you may be penalized
7 George Bush or Dan Quayle: Abbr.
8 Biol. course
9 Rival of Walter and Byron
10 Home to Jesper
11 Parred, perhaps
12 Ann Landers's home state
13 ___ Express
18 Ryder Cup team position: Abbr.
25 Cinemax rival: Abbr.
27 Not doing well on a ship
29 Obit bit
31 Tony Jacklin's nat.
32 Let 'er ___ (hit a long drive)
33 State of anger
34 "The next round's ___!" (clubhouse announcement)
35 Snooze
36 "___ boy!" (maternity ward cry)
37 Shots that never happened, wink-wink
40 Command to a dog to attack
42 Holy man: Abbr.
43 Brewski
44 Deodorant brand Soft & ___
47 One-hit wonder?
50 1991 British Open champ Baker-Finch
52 Saudi ___
53 New England drinks
54 Systems many M.D.'s work under
58 Golf course measurements
59 Glistened
60 School headaches
61 First name of a legend in women's golf
62 Woods, to many kids
64 Young fellas
65 Troubles
67 Standout
71 Elder of the golf course
72 Narcissist's feature

ANSWER, PAGE 80

THIS AND THAT

Some noted golf twosomes.

ACROSS

1 With 14-Across, salvages par
6 Driving range purchase
11 Prefix with angle
14 See 1-Across
15 "Shaq" of the NBA
16 "The Twilight Zone" creator Serling
17 Match play result
19 Hit with, as a club
20 Pernice, Jr. of golf
21 Gives a quote
22 Tournament coverers
24 Flight parts
27 Reaction to a Daly drive
28 Avoid the worst from a greenside bunker
35 Reno-___ Open
38 "There you have it!"
39 Golf ___
40 Genetically-coded stuff, for short
41 Taps
44 Title for many members of the LPGA Tour
45 Big name in razors
47 Swing impeder, sometimes
48 Relaxes, as pressure
50 Kind of golf course
53 Prez after Jimmy
54 Cold cut choice
58 Captain of the first six U.S. Ryder Cup teams
61 Sacred mountain of the Orient
64 "___ I do that?" (comment after a shank)
65 ___-American (Payne Stewart, at SMU)
66 Tactic used approaching hard greens
70 Enjoyed the 19th hole, maybe

71 Has the ___ (plays first)
72 Par five possibility
73 Tiger, to Earl
74 U.S. and British
75 Curvy letters

DOWN

1 Gogel and namesakes
2 Take ___ at (try to hit, as the green)
3 Belief of Hinduism
4 Adam's madam
5 Comprehend
6 ___ fide
7 North on the links
8 ___ play through (allows to pass)
9 Murphy's ___ (it reigns on the golf course)

10 Like some fairways
11 Not tricky, as a putt
12 Flag-sewing woman
13 March 15th or April 13th
18 Coach's helper: Abbr.
23 Best Picture nominee of 1981
25 "Mind if ___ first?" (opening hole question)
26 Surfing hazard
27 Distraction to putters
29 180-degree switch
30 Showed nervousness
31 Fall into ___ sleep
32 Bits of resistance
33 Sported, as the green jacket

34 Loch ___ Monster
35 Sandy trouble
36 Not pro-
37 Gary or Corey
42 ___ impasse (stalemated)
43 ___ course record
46 Measurement of a golf course's size
49 It's between the U.S. and the U.K.
51 Head ___ (big boss)
52 "Tell ___ your own words ..."
55 Lead ___ life (suffer)
56 Director Cecil B. De ___
57 Lazes around
58 Jay of the Tour
59 High voice
60 Canada's ___ Abbey Golf Course
61 A player may get one for misbehaving
62 Atop
63 Containers for cookies
67 Use one foot
68 Actor Billy ___ Williams
69 College dorm chiefs: Abbr.

EASY RYDER

There is no I in T-E-A-M.

ACROSS

1 Sluman or Maggert
5 Gimme's distance, perhaps
9 Hitting
14 Home to one of the PGA Tours
15 "Sleepless in Seattle" director Ephron
16 Members of the gallery may do it
17 New England city that hosted the first Ryder Cup in 1927
19 ___ different tune (changed one's mind)
20 He's just keeping his head above water
22 ___ tea
23 George Bush once headed it
26 Exclamation from Langer
27 Tre + tre
29 Actress ___ Dawn Chong
30 In a perfect world
32 Show up at the tournament
34 Pate or Elkington
35 Scott on the links
38 Orlando, to Tiger
39 Biological group
40 Recipe amts.
43 Padraig Harrington's home
45 "Show ___ you did that!"
46 Fight it out in match play
48 Like LPGA Tour members
49 Nelson Mandela's party
50 It oozes from trees
52 Golf bag contents
53 Day before many PGA Tour events start: Abbr.
54 Sunshine cracker
56 Jones's legacy
59 Make ___ of (really botch)
61 Site of the 1985, 1989, 1993, and 2002 Ryder Cups
65 They might contain golf shops
66 Get better
67 Brainstorming product
68 Let slide
69 "Ditto!"
70 Truck brand

DOWN

1 Face part
2 That, to Olazabal
3 Kind of pine
4 Bit of trivia
5 One might land on your golf ball
6 First name on the Tour
7 Ability to be loaned money: Abbr.
8 Quick animals
9 Summertime coolers: Abbr.
10 Like Jenny Chuasiriporn's surname
11 U.S. Ryder Cup captain for 1999's memorable comeback win
12 With 35-Down, Greece borderer
13 Went to a swap meet
18 Overcome, as a lead
21 Enjoys the harvest
23 Check alternative
24 "Tell ___ the judge!"
25 Golfer whose likeness appears on top of the Ryder Cup
28 "___ breaking to the left" (golf commentator's sentence)
31 Navratilova rival
33 Pole for Native Americans
35 See 12-Down
36 Place to crash for the night
37 A divot may contain some
39 Eye brightness
41 Warsaw resident
42 Liselotte Neumann's nat.
44 Pal of Goosen
45 Measurement for Nick Faldo
46 Grand ___ (island off Florida's coast)
47 Zoo resident
48 Like putts that come up way short
51 Golf cart routes
52 Prepare vegetables in a healthy way
55 Cold European capital
57 New York stadium
58 Like David Duval
60 Compass dir. opposite NNE
62 Govt. agency involved in approving medicines
63 ___ room
64 Talk and talk

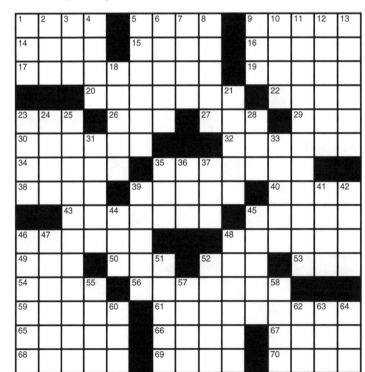

ANSWER, PAGE 84

HOW TO IMPROVE AT GOLF

If all these fail, try lessons.

ACROSS

1 What you shot
6 Life
10 Pro ___
14 Name between Edgar and Poe
15 Nature's tape recorder?
16 Up ___ good
17 It can help you improve at golf
19 Putt's movement
20 Mark Calcavecchia's is named Eric
21 Get ___ of (grab)
22 Home to Ayako Okamoto
23 Pig ___ poke
24 Diving bird
25 It can help you improve at golf
32 How Tiger stands
33 ___ times (the past)
34 Rogers or Orbison
36 Doesn't keep pace
37 Drinks moonshine
38 Before: Prefix
39 It may be favorable for a golfer
40 Ridiculous
41 Astrological sign for Ayako Okamoto
42 They can help you improve at golf
45 Baseball ___ (topper for many golfers)
46 Short story of one's life
47 1995 U.S. Open champ
50 Witch trial city
53 1975 U.S. Open champ Graham
56 ___ vera
57 They can help you improve at golf
59 Goes bad
60 Baldwin of "The Hunt for Red October"
61 Flood stopper
62 Proofreading mark that means "let it stand"
63 Very hard studier
64 Gives the appearance

DOWN

1 Tools with teeth
2 Nile queen, for short
3 Actress Lena of "Havana"
4 Ball washer adjunct
5 Improve, as one's links performance
6 Number of PGA Championships Arnold Palmer won
7 Greenpeace concern: Abbr.
8 Provided footwear for
9 1973 British Open winner Weiskopf
10 Penalty ___
11 Drive feature, perhaps
12 Sole
13 Game played with equines
18 "Did I do ___?" (golfer's sigh)
22 ___ pro (join the Tour)
23 Woosnam and Baker-Finch
24 Seemingly forever
25 Tartan pattern
26 Maltbie of the Tour
27 Dubuque resident
28 Barely hold (onto), as a lead
29 Garden tool
30 Mr. Els
31 Students take them in class
32 The whole shebang
35 "Natch!"
37 Make incisions
38 Jason's ship
40 "Terrible" czar
41 The tiger and the walrus
43 Most unfriendly
44 Cain's victim
47 Course standards
48 Bunches and bunches
49 Participate on election day
50 Missile's spot
51 ___ Corner (Masters stretch)
52 You'll need some to get a hole-in-one
53 1997 PGA Championship winner
54 Utah city
55 Employs
57 Spotted
58 Driving tool

ANSWER, PAGE 86

37

ALL MIXED UP

"D BATTERY" is "TED TRYBA." You do the rest.

ACROSS

1 ___ Mountain, Georgia
5 It may get on your golf shoes
8 ___ Braid, member of golf's "Triumvirate"
13 Psych ending
14 Where some watch golf from
15 With one's mouth open
16 SHUT TALON
18 More achy
19 ___ Angeles
20 Apple or blueberry
21 "Much ___ About Nothing"
23 Hawaii's Mauna ___
24 Prominent first name on the LPGA Tour
26 "Do ___ others ..."
28 Full of power
31 Meaning-changing word
33 Spanish linkster Uresti
36 "___ is a terrible thing to waste"
37 Stench
38 Beatles hit "Love ___"
39 Tee, for instance
40 SKIP ERA
43 Oklahoma city
44 Like fine cheese
46 Black and Yellow
47 1979 film "The Lady ___"
49 Lee of food
50 Jack Nicklaus's has caddied for him
51 Sam and J.C.
52 Shout to a horse or a putt that you want to stop
54 Garcia's buddy
56 From ___ Z
58 Soap ingredient
60 In ___-win situation
61 Not masc.
64 Was a rude member of the gallery
66 AND I FLOCK
69 Mr. Agassi
70 Rowboat movers
71 Fails to keep up
72 Ascended
73 ___-cat (wintertime vehicle)
74 "Now ___ it!"

DOWN

1 Dan of the Tour
2 First name in Japanese golf
3 Zeroes, in soccer
4 Letter with curves
5 Place to stay for the night
6 Creepy flyer
7 Quigley of the Senior PGA Tour
8 Buha or Caron of the Tour
9 In the past
10 AROMA MAKER
11 Sword used in the Olympics
12 Word appearing twice after "Que," in a famous song
14 Prop for a clown
17 Defeats
22 1932 and 1934 major winner Olin ___
24 Four-time winner on the 1958 Tour Venturi
25 Jones of film
27 Kite on the course
28 Daddies
29 ___ Asian PGA Tour
30 DOES IT GROW
32 Word said after missing a two-foot putt
34 Tallied one's score
35 Routes for coupes
37 Cookie brand
41 John Feinstein piece
42 ___ clubs (playing card, or nickname for 30-Down?)
45 "Zip-A-Dee-Doo-___"
48 Prefix that means "new"
51 Makes a putt
53 The ___ days (yesteryear)
55 On a large scale
56 "A guy walks into ___ ..." (joke start)
57 Author Morrison
59 "Dukes of Hazzard" character
61 Hole marker
62 Border, as of the fairway
63 Not quite all
65 Before
67 Welsh wonder Woosnam
68 Big name in the ring

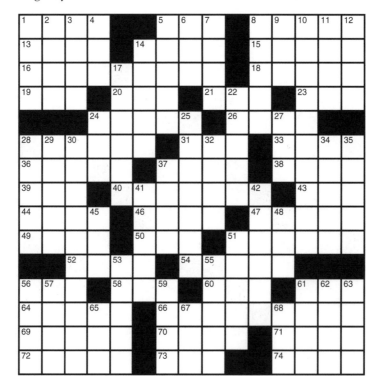

ANSWER, PAGE 88

MY CUP RUNNETH OVER

Celebrating the Solheim.

ACROSS

1 With 5-Across, Europe's team captain in the 2000 Solheim Cup
5 See 1-Across
9 Junior players
13 1995 movie "Mr. Holland's ___"
14 Switzerland's capital
15 Stuck in ___
16 Site of the first Solheim Cup in 1990
19 Before
20 Suffix meaning "followers"
21 Good putting ability or strong arms
22 Andrew and Pierre: Abbr.
23 Use a wedge
25 U.S. team captain for the 1996 and 1998 Solheim Cups
30 Ernie who can't play in a Solheim cup
33 ___ acid
34 Thousand ___, California
35 Tournament results, player reactions, etc.

37 "May ___ excused?"
38 Prefix with angle
39 ___ time
40 Golf bag feature
42 He scored a double eagle in the 1985 U.S. Open
43 ___ mashie (old name for a six-iron)
45 King, in Marseilles
46 Solheim's most famous club
48 Breadth
50 Donkey or burro
51 "Stars and Stripes Forever" composer
54 Volcano's outpouring
56 Place to slim down

59 Europe's only undefeated player in the 1996 Solheim Cup
63 He finally won a major in 1992
64 Religious offshoots
65 Light
66 "Dukes of Hazzard" policeman
67 Sore
68 Bush or Clinton: Abbr.

DOWN

1 Pineapple brand
2 On ___ with (equal to, as a golfer?)
3 Mr. Skywalker
4 Ending for Japan
5 Those without a set of clubs must do it

6 Times of yore
7 Beethoven's "Sonata ___ Minor"
8 "Runaway" singer Shannon
9 Mr. Solheim
10 Eye part
11 Ranch hand
12 Percentage of fairways hit or number of putts per green
14 "Blame It on the ___ Nova"
17 Prefix with glycerine
18 Dolt
22 Dictionary entry: Abbr.
23 Preference
24 Tap-___ (short putts)
25 The slammer
26 Yellowish-brown color

27 San ___ (home to Mission Bay Golf Resort)
28 "What's goin' on?" reply
29 LPGA Tour player Pearce
31 Allow to attack
32 Gabriel Hjertstedt, for example
36 Clairvoyant
41 Bullies might pick on them
42 One who is busy in Apr.
43 Florin or Ginter of the LPGA Tour
44 Solheim Cup nos.
47 Works on the cart path
49 Golf star ineligible for the Solheim Cup
51 "For Pete's ___!"
52 "Come right ___!"
53 Golden Rule word
54 ___ Lomond (site of the 2000 Solheim Cup)
55 Highfalutin'
56 Commotion
57 Peel an apple
58 Alcott and Fruhwirth
60 Solid ___ rock
61 "Just a ___!"
62 Tree fluid

HAIL TO THE CHIEF

And to his tournament.

ACROSS

1 He was the Honorary Chairman of the 1996 Presidents Cup
5 Bucket
9 Thomas Bjorn is one
13 Where the Nobel Peace Prize is awarded
14 Drifting
16 Not over par, not under par
17 Great windfall
18 He was the Honorary Chairman of the inaugural Presidents Cup
20 Runner-up to North at the 1985 U.S. Open
22 State that's home to Mark O'Meara: Abbr.
23 "___ got to get a new putter!" (green excuse)
24 Big fuss
27 Wore away
29 Captain of the U.S. team in the 1996 Presidents Cup
34 "___ down!" (shout to a ball that looks long)
35 It might be unstoppable
36 Toms or Duval
40 Dan who won twice on the 1986 Tour

42 Club-making company
44 ___ double life
45 He famously never won the U.S. Open
47 Tournament director's concern
49 ___ Tin Tin
50 Three-time captain of the International Team in the Presidents Cup
53 Bag toter
56 "Do you ___ ball anywhere?"
57 Mo. of the Masters
58 Actor Stephen of "Interview With the Vampire"
60 Norse god for whom a day of the week is named

62 Former captain of the U.S. team in the Presidents Cup
65 Illinois neighbor
69 Ending for switch
70 It should be replaced
71 Many a Tour event
72 High schoolers take them
73 Tiny bits
74 Cold War side

DOWN

1 May or Tway
2 ___ Tour (Bob Hope event)
3 ___-mo replay
4 VIP
5 Call over the loudspeaker
6 "I give it ___!" (contest judge's phrase)

7 Nat. where you can play at Caesarea
8 Lie affecter, in fall
9 C followers
10 Dodge
11 Willingness to attempt a risky shot
12 Put the kibosh on, as a comeback attempt
15 Tour player Fulton
19 Had the gumption
21 Part of many Presidents Cup scores
24 Door fastenings
25 Constellation with a belt
26 ___ green (ready to putt)
28 Like some exams

30 Part of a lowercase J
31 Durban-born golf star
32 Bob Hope or Jamie Farr
33 "Last but not ___ ..."
37 Bit of Frost
38 "He's a diamond in the rough," for example
39 Five-time Tour winner Edwards
41 Certain resident of Finland
43 To the ___ degree (extremely)
46 John ___ Classic
48 Just average
51 Business tendency
52 Pennsylvania course that hosted the 1971 and 1981 U.S. Opens
53 Water hazards, sometimes
54 Beethoven's "Fidelio" is one
55 Whether ___
59 Keep ___ (persist)
60 Walked upon
61 Drives, as a ball
63 Smart columnist Marilyn ___ Savant
64 School founded by Thomas Jefferson
66 ___-Locka, Florida
67 Like some slow greens
68 Year, to Miguel Angel Jimenez

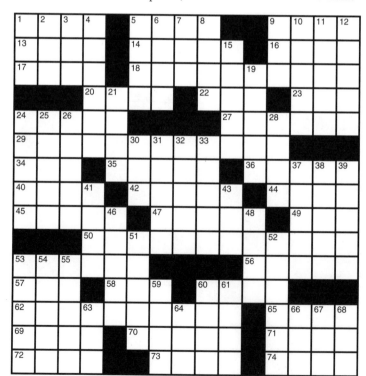

ANSWER, PAGE 92

THE SHOT

Golf's rarest shot, that is.

ACROSS

1 1969 PGA leading money winner Frank
6 Was up a few strokes
9 Greenskeeper or caddie
12 Vijay Singh's ancestral homeland
13 Bob who sang "Night Moves"
15 Madison or Pennsylvania: Abbr.
16 "The Shot"
18 It might enclose a driving range
19 Letter after kay
20 Golf course
21 Suffix with theater or church
23 Stopped, as a golf ball
24 FBI employees: Abbr.
25 "Zinger" Azinger
26 Hard wood
27 Press tent worker
29 Breadth

32 Golfer who made "The Shot" at the 1985 U.S. Open
35 Steve Case's co.
37 ___ lead (be winning)
39 Tic-tac-toe win
40 Go wrong
42 More than cry
43 Golfer who made "The Shot" at the 1999 British Masters
46 "Jane ___"
47 Ed or Richard of film fame
49 Dream result on a par three
51 Hard work
52 Kiss partner
54 ___ Oil Treatment
57 Shot, as a score
59 Give a speech
60 Part of many a nest egg

61 Fuss
62 Golfer who made "The Shot" at the 1935 Masters
65 Where one lives: Abbr.
66 PGA Tour calendar item
67 They should be bent during your swing
68 College dorm overseers
69 Not merely -er
70 Likely to talk back

DOWN

1 Marks, as time
2 ___ Gay (WWII plane)
3 Person of age
4 Tease gently
5 City where 1-Across was born

6 Signs that you need a new roof
7 Brunch items
8 Neighbor of Md.
9 Australian golfer who made "The Shot" at the 2000 Compaq Open
10 ___ par
11 Golfers might make them to liven the round up
13 Mailed
14 Takes back, as the lead
17 Number of majors Tom Watson won
22 Hole ___
25 ___-tournament favorite
26 Pitch ___ putt
27 "Stop, horse!"
28 Crowd's sound
29 Golf course admonishments

30 A.A. Milne's bear
31 Another name for "The Shot"
33 Corn comes on them
34 It follows dot
36 Soap ingredient
38 Shorten
41 A golfer puts it in the ground
44 Major British export
45 Conference site of 1945
48 Fish eggs
50 They assist judges
52 Legendary golf course designer Robert ___ Jones
53 Sunrise direction
54 Golf shoe specifications
55 Golf shot hinderers, frequently
56 Kind of violet
57 Jamie of golf patronage
58 Brain product
59 Small bills
63 Adam's lady
64 Santa ___ (city southeast of L.A.)

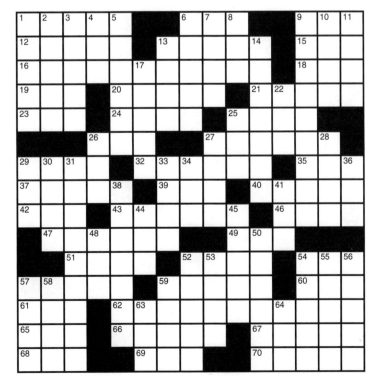

ANSWER, PAGE 94

WHAT ABOUT BOB?

Few have done more for golf than he.

ACROSS

1 1986 U.S. Women's Open winner Geddes
5 Knickerbockers don't cover them
10 The basics
14 Sleep like ___
15 Scorecard sum
16 Wood cousin
17 Golfing buddy of Bob Hope
19 World's longest river
20 Like those with the yips
21 Major-winner Lawson or Sally
23 Swing maker
26 Watch
27 Tiger often hits it
28 Neighbor of Syr.
29 Aussie star Grady
31 Baseball stat
33 Golf cart need
35 Fuzzy sweater
37 Short Line and Reading, in Monopoly: Abbr.
39 50% of a famous name in golf
41 Hole measurement

42 Ending for somer
44 Actress Spelling of "Beverly Hills, 90210"
46 ___ up
47 ___ Senior Classic
48 Curtis Strange won it twice in a row
50 Extreme ending
52 Had the upper hand
54 "___ we all?"
55 Charged particle
57 The odds against scoring one on a given hole are 42,942 to 1
59 Miss a putt, say
61 Prefix with conservative
62 Taker of many mulligans
64 Like Isao Aoki or T.C. Chen

66 ___-day (kind of multivitamin)
67 President who Bob Hope often golfed with
72 Keeps from swelling
73 Severe
74 Georgia-born Jerry
75 School event
76 Campers sleep in them
77 Dutch cheese that comes in red wax

DOWN

1 Quick punch
2 The Jack Nicklaus of boxing, so to speak
3 "Smoking or ___?"
4 They come in dozens
5 Go wrong

6 "Confessions of a ___" (Bob Hope's golf memoir)
7 ___-bitsy
8 Snare a thief
9 With cleverness
10 Is not, in dialect
11 Bob Hope played in it in 1950
12 Univs.
13 Show contempt
18 Be a good member of the gallery
22 Mark McCormack's company
23 Having the right to putt first
24 Attacked
25 "I tell jokes to pay ___": Bob Hope
27 Future U.S. Women's Open champ, maybe
30 Central points

32 Laid-back Tour player Lietzke
34 Bob Hope, often
36 Horse cousin
38 R-V links
40 Woman's name that means "peace"
43 Having the skill
45 Having as a hobby
49 Abraham's wife, in the Bible
51 ___-bo (fitness craze)
53 Bob Hope ___ Classic (longtime PGA Tour event)
55 "Did ___ right?" (question to a golf instructor)
56 Pound part
58 Wave's top
60 Places to skate
63 Some greens play this way
64 Strong ___ ox
65 Casual refusal
68 Ending for Manhattan
69 Pocketful of cash
70 Seventh Greek letter
71 Michael Stipe's band

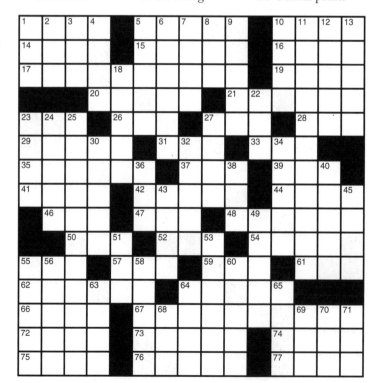

ANSWER, PAGE 81

STARTING ON THE SEVENTEENTH

But not the seventeenth hole.

ACROSS

1 1916 U.S. Open and U.S. Amateur winner Chick
6 They cover golf tournaments
11 Fairway-obscuring phenomenon
14 Fairly free of mistakes, as a round
15 "___ you clever!"
16 "Ah, now I get it!"
17 It determines who plays
20 Dir. on a compass
21 ___ Hill, Rochester (site of the 1989 U.S. Open)
22 Money for Langer and Olazabal
23 Nineteenth hole feature
25 "I can make ___" (gimme taker's statement)
27 Greatly-reduced swing
32 Women of the house
35 Prepare to remove, as one's golf shoes
36 Crowd-pleasing rarities
37 "St. Matthew Passion" composer

38 Work like ___
39 Keep one's roommate awake, maybe
40 Old Testament book
41 Venturi and others
42 It's used in gumbo
43 Playing ___
44 Prior to
45 Words on a marshal's sign
47 ___ Brae, Mass. (site of the 1919 U.S. Open)
48 No longer playing: Abbr.
49 Sailing
52 To's partner
54 Make after expenses
57 Serious scorecard blemishes

62 It holds a lot of coffee
63 Shot blockers, often
64 Davies of the LPGA Tour
65 3 ___ 2 (match score)
66 Definitely not golf weather
67 Place to get a BLT

DOWN

1 Attys.
2 You, on the Bayou
3 "There oughta be ___ against that!"
4 Zippo
5 "Star Wars" missile shield: Abbr.
6 Chichen Itza resident
7 Actor Estrada

8 Thomas Bjorn's country: Abbr.
9 Verb suffix
10 "You're in for ___!"
11 Golfing group, often
12 Cry from a duffer
13 They smile on the lucky
18 Links alert
19 ___ of bounds
23 Military prisons
24 Chowed down
25 Year of ___ (1984 or 1996, to the Chinese)
26 Piece of equipment for a greenskeeper
27 Have the yips
28 See 29-Down
29 With 28-Down, having birdied the first hole

30 LPGA leading money winner for 1976 and 1977
31 Golfers sometimes fib about it
32 Frequent past sponsor of Senior PGA Tour events
33 Word in many golf course names
34 Have a part of, as the lead
37 Headwear for Monica Lewinsky
39 Like bad milk
43 "Nice job!"
45 Gallon fourths
46 "No ___!" ("Fine!")
47 Place to crash
49 Bluish-green
50 Make the ___ (start the back nine)
51 Trap stuff
52 Get outta town
53 Skip this week's tournament
54 Nine, in Nuremberg
55 "Jane ___"
56 Ruler until 1917
58 Web address
59 Carolina's ___ Dee River
60 ___ Tom Morris (golf legend)
61 Moo goo ___ pan (Chinese dish)

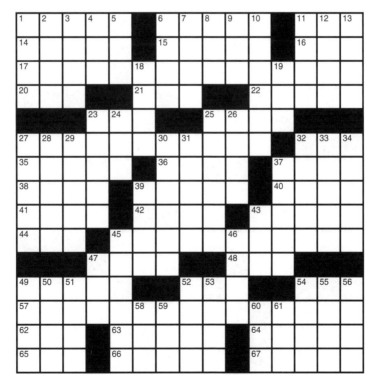

OUT OF AFRICA

South Africa, that is.

ACROSS

1 Certain musical note
6 Miss, as an easy putt
10 Mr. Azinger
14 Scent from the kitchen
15 ___ close second (lost by just a stroke)
16 "Rules of Golf" org.
17 He won the Masters at age 42
19 Sounds from Scrooge
20 Tupperware tops
21 Iron-___ (some patches)
22 Zero, in soccer
24 South African star
25 Letters after business names
26 Compact ___
30 He never played the PGA Tour, but has several victories on the Senior PGA Tour
34 South African star who won twice on the 1993 PGA Tour
37 Missing without permission
38 Not quite a mansion
39 Home to a lion
40 Gone up in the rankings
42 Best Actress winner of 1992 Thompson

43 It's a looker
44 Crenshaw and Hogan
45 David of South African golf
46 Tour star struck by lightning as an amateur
50 Site of British Open wins by Justin Leonard and Mark Calcavecchia
51 Popular potato chip brand
52 1,000,000, casually
55 The PGA of tennis, so to speak
57 One ___ time (how golfers drive)
58 It's carried by singers
59 Long story

62 He won four British Opens in a nine-year span
65 "Once ___ a time ..."
66 "That's ___ know!"
67 Differing
68 Dog-catcher's equipment
69 ___ up
70 Only person to win the U.S. Amateur three times in a row

DOWN

1 ___ putt
2 Shaky-looking
3 Some members of the nobility
4 Alcott and Fruhwirth
5 ___-in (putt of inches)

6 You can be penalized if your practice swing hits one
7 ___ the ball up
8 ___-iron
9 Holler "fore"
10 Like some golf courses
11 Solid ___ rock
12 Post-shank utterance
13 ___ Palmas, Spain
18 Like some putts or golf courses
23 70-Across, to many kids
25 Last three letters of many chemical elements
27 Average guy
28 Clique members
29 Use, as a table
30 Yonder female

31 Lowest male voice
32 Wonder
33 "Am ___ the green?"
34 On the ball
35 Section of cake
36 Fail to be truthful with
40 Ump
41 Verbal suffix
42 Ending for north or west
44 Like a golf club after an angry player is done with it
45 Hat named for a city in Morocco
47 Des Moines residents
48 Succeed at an auction
49 Stick around
52 Lots, to Olazabal
53 Signed, as a contract
54 Creepy looks
56 Blind as ___
57 Knowing how
58 Famous Hollywood dog
59 ___ City Challenge (South African event won three times by 45-Across)
60 Repeat word for word
61 Achieved, as a par
63 "Well done!"
64 Kind of score golfers want

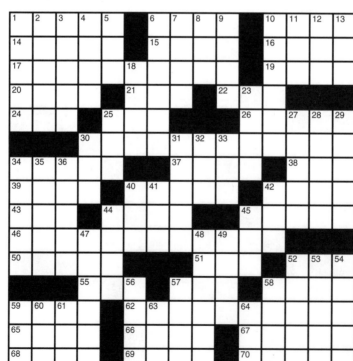

ANSWER, PAGE 85

SKIN DEEP

A quiz about a quality quartet.

ACROSS

1 Gogel and others
6 Aussie star Stephenson
9 Hits from near the green
14 "I'm such an ___!" (cry of a frustrated golfer)
15 Golden years money
16 Vietnam's capital
17 Skins Game winner of 1997
19 See 49-Across
20 "___ got a bad lie"
21 A trailers
23 Fruit associated with tequila
24 Lousy linksters
28 Starchy side dish food
30 Birdbrain
31 Plot of land
32 Like shots that go in the water
34 "Heat" director Michael
36 Jane or John
37 Belief of about a billion
39 Shrill shout
41 Came to a close
43 LPGA Tour player Dahllof
44 Ring ___ (seem familiar)

46 Org. that oversees some golf tournaments
47 Becomes bogged down
49 With 19-Across, four-time winner on the 1985 Senior PGA Tour
50 Communally owned
52 Bogey score, sometimes
53 Career grand ___ (accomplishment of Tiger's)
54 Payne Stewart's alma mater
56 Ryder Cup team: Abbr.
58 Major location
60 Solheim and others
62 "___ appétit!"
64 Gallery noise

65 ___ once (not how a foursome should putt)
67 Extra-valuable hole
72 Superman portrayer Christopher
73 ___ out a win (barely emerge victorious)
74 Renter's agreement
75 English county northeast of London
76 One of 100 in Wash.
77 Way of golfing

DOWN

1 Harvard rival
2 Fracas
3 Director Burton
4 Drinking toast
5 Elkington or Pate

6 Mr. Furyk
7 Mecca resident
8 Ms. Lopez
9 First name in revolts
10 PGA Tour ___ of Fame
11 Former Skins Game locale
12 Frost works
13 Is the dad
18 Food jazzer-uppers
22 River blocker
24 Miami-___ (Florida county)
25 New England college, for short
26 His 18th-hole birdie in the 1999 Skins Game was worth $410,000
27 City of witch trials
29 Ancient Central Americans

33 Love on the links
35 Stop the crook
37 "___ you!" (challenge to a golfer contemplating a risky shot)
38 Hjorth of the LPGA Tour
40 Skirt crease
42 Water, in Quebec
45 1964 British Open champ Tony
48 Show, as confidence
51 Long sandwich
53 End of play, often
54 Give a fright
55 Barge draggers
57 February flowers
59 Laura Davies and Se Ri Pak, once
61 ___ par
63 Pop in the microwave
66 State where 49-Across was born: Abbr.
68 Some keep their scorecards in it
69 Letter after jay
70 Bermuda or Hawaii: Abbr.
71 Word seen in wedding announcements

GET A JOB

On the course, of course.

ACROSS

1 Hunk of meat
5 John who won three times on the 1992 PGA Tour
9 Occasions for the National Guard
14 Part of a country: Abbr.
15 Try to tempt
16 Video game pioneer
17 Number of times Tom Kite won a major
18 "Kill ___ killed" (match play mentality?)
19 "Golf is more fun than walking ___ in a strange place, but not much": Buddy Hackett
20 They're strived for
22 Intentionally leave a putt short
24 Get a look at
25 Looper superviser
29 Since
30 Earthquake's shake
34 He tells you when to drive
37 Put ___ into (frighten)
38 Expensive entree
39 Bit of wine
41 Vicinity
42 Tiger's is astronomical
45 Lesson-giver, often
48 Not very nice-sounding
49 Dad's sis
50 He makes sure the rough isn't too rough
56 1200, in Roman numerals
59 ___-fi
60 Golf cart hummer
61 Sand trap, slangily
63 Pessimistic
66 Wanders aimlessly
67 First letter in Athens
68 Angel's instrument
69 "Sit ___!" (insult from the Fonz)
70 Grab and run
71 "How could I have missed ___?" (golf course lament)
72 Have-___ (the poor)

DOWN

1 Not overly emotional
2 ___ hand (help)
3 Like nine-iron shots
4 Bakery output
5 Not away
6 "___ Town"
7 Heavenly body
8 Ship parts
9 Course cops
10 "Make ___ double!" (nineteenth hole request)
11 Trees on many courses
12 Risk/reward hole feature, often
13 Team, as in the Ryder Cup
21 Tall tale teller
23 Prefix with "girl" or "boy"
26 Tavern on "The Simpsons"
27 Nick Price or Mark McNulty
28 Summary
31 1965 PGA Championship winner Dave
32 Cookie with its name stamped on it
33 Stephen of "The Crying Game"
34 Visited the post office, maybe
35 Snack in Sonora
36 Has ___ putt (needs some heroics on the green)
38 By way of
40 Word golfers don't like in their scores
43 He quiets down the gallery
44 Part of GE
46 Dirty
47 Bingo call
51 High iron
52 Goad
53 It has keys and pedals
54 Break up, informally
55 Doesn't play
56 Some entrepreneurs have them: Abbr.
57 Padraig Harrington or Gary Orr
58 Canaveral or Good Hope
62 Half a dance
64 Cry from cheerleaders
65 Golden years money, for short

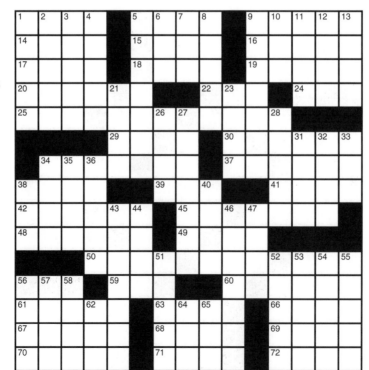

ANSWER, PAGE 89

FOR THE BIRDS

Swallow your pride and solve this one.

ACROSS

1 Each
5 Recipe instruction
9 Beauty's mate
14 El ___ (Sergio Garcia)
15 Big mistake
16 Reddish-brown color
17 They curve sharply
19 It's on the card
20 "___ to remember something about ..."
21 Like John Daly
23 "___ gotta try that!"
24 Rare deuces
29 Tway or May
32 ___-mo camera
33 ___ roll (doing well)
34 One way to run
36 "___ life!"
38 Booster jet
42 Veteran Tour player
44 Another term for a double bogey
46 "___ I said before ..."

47 Feature of some approach shots
49 "My word!"
50 Korean brand of car
52 www.emory.___
53 Part of DOS
54 His best finish on the 2000 PGA Tour was 3rd at the Nissan Open
60 ___-square (match play score)
61 Baseball's Ripken
62 ___ up (concedes a hole)
66 State where you can play at the Boise Ranch Golf Course
69 Like some clubs
72 Big name for shutterbugs
73 Money for Olazabal or Montgomerie

74 Helen's city
75 Oozes
76 Gumbo or goulash
77 ___ Christian Andersen

DOWN

1 Beatles song "___ Love Her"
2 One of twelve popes
3 Not repeatedly
4 Looked for one's ball in the rough, perhaps
5 ___-cone
6 ___ far (like overhit shots)
7 Rorschach test feature
8 Jones of the LPGA Tour
9 Token transportation
10 Letters in Einstein's equation

11 Like some pots on the stove
12 Bring food to
13 Green-obscurers, sometimes
18 Doctors' gp.
22 Prefix that means "earth"
25 "Rules of Golf" org.
26 Say "Gesundheit!"
27 1998 cartoon movie featuring Woody Allen's voice
28 Wound cover
29 ___ California
30 Arabian peninsula country
31 Woody's surname on "Cheers"
35 Golfer's pants color, sometimes
37 Tolerate
39 They hang from ball washers

40 Donkey's cry
41 They're long against a hole-in-one
43 G ___ "golf"
45 "E pluribus ___"
48 Leave loudly in a car
51 Part of the NFL
54 They cause tournament delays
55 1950s tune
56 Jay Don ___ of the PGA Tour
57 Goes nuts
58 Get better, maybe
59 Last hole on the front of the course
63 Aloe ___
64 "The dismal science": Abbr.
65 "The ___ the limit!"
67 Use one leg
68 Carry-___ (some airline baggage)
70 Material from a mine
71 Female in a pasture

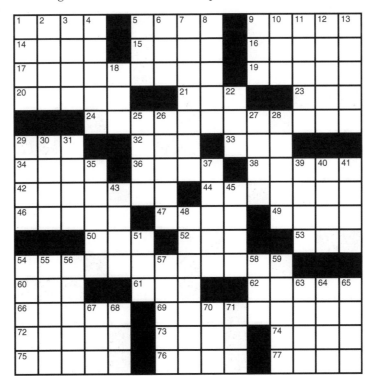

WHO SAID THAT?

From the quote, guess the speaker.

ACROSS

1 Quigley of the Senior PGA Tour
5 Perform a ball-owner's task
9 Blind as ___
13 "Famous" cookiemaker
14 Mr. Irwin
15 Fancy wheels
16 "It took me 17 years to get 3,000 hits in baseball. I did it in one afternoon on a golf course."
18 "We're ___ your side!"
19 Choir voice
20 Competition
22 Half a bikini
25 Actor Chaney
26 Letters in personal ads
27 "I made the putt! Awesome!"
28 A player may seek it from an official
30 Like a bug in a rug
32 "___ event ..."
33 You, in olden times
36 Clubs may employ them
39 Up ___ good
40 Bar Harbor's location
41 California valley
42 Part of PGA
43 Many NYC dwellings: Abbr.
44 Former Defense Secretary Bill
45 Mr., to Langer
47 Risk-___ hole
48 Eisenhower's nickname
50 "What did ___ wrong?" (question during a lesson)
52 It's comprised of atoms: Abbr.
53 Bob of golf
54 Hook feature
56 First murder victim
58 Like golfers who throw their clubs
59 "Ninety percent of putts left short don't go in."
64 ___ Lee of cakes
65 British or Canadian
66 Ryder Cup ___
67 North of the course
68 Hits with, as a club
69 Walkman maker

DOWN

1 Lah-di-___ (pretentious)
2 "I ___ Camera"
3 ___-exempt (Tour status)
4 "___ silly question ..."
5 "___ it?" ("So?")
6 1973 Masters winner Tommy
7 ___-mo camera
8 One of four French kings
9 "This is ___ big misunderstanding!"
10 "The Lord answers my prayers everywhere but on the course."
11 Love, Italian-style
12 Lema and Jacklin
17 Building for bowling
18 Shakespeare's river
21 Hot topic
22 Company that makes water filters
23 Former Attorney General Janet and family
24 "Because of the suit I was wearing, I couldn't get a good pivot on the swing."
29 Hole-___
31 "You can shut ___!" (comment to someone laughing at your missed two-footer?)
33 ___-in (gimme)
34 Take a swing
35 Light switch settings
37 Highbrow entertainment
38 Mr. Lyle, or like bunkers
40 Lunn of the LPGA Tour
44 Tiger Woods or Tom Hanks
46 Ready for plucking
47 Round-___ (some tournaments)
48 "___ far, far better thing ...": Dickens
49 Holy book for some
51 "The joke's ___!"
52 Andrew of golf
55 ___ at three under (fail to birdie)
57 ___ through (allows a faster group by)
60 Photo-___
61 ___ Speedwagon
62 Reacted to "Fore!"
63 Ms. Alcott

48

ACE!

One-hit wonders.

ACROSS

1 Creatures that make people shriek
5 Penne or fusilli
10 Carries around, as a set of clubs
14 ___ Sea (world's fourth-biggest lake)
15 "Your lights ___"
16 Like ___ (with skill)
17 At the 1992 Masters, he became the only player in the tournament's history to ace hole #4
19 Leg section
20 ___ under par (score after a first-hole birdie)
21 Prefix with present
22 Putting on a show
24 Fix a golf shoe
26 Ocean one team must cross to play the Walker Cup: Abbr.
27 They're aced very rarely—by Tommy Nakajima at the 1998 Chinuchi Crowns tournament in Japan, for instance
34 Mocking look
37 Kind of sentence

38 ___-di-dah (pretentious)
39 Come ___ end (finish)
40 ___-trained
41 Get higher
42 Intensive care unit tubes
43 Asian city where you can practice at the Lang Ha Golf Driving Range
44 Borscht ingredients
45 He won both his PGA Championships with the help of holes-in-one
48 Golf cart need
49 Biannual team tourneys, casually
53 Se Ri Pak's home: Abbr.

56 Chanel of perfume
58 "___ Married an Axe Murderer"
59 53, in Ancient Rome
60 European Senior PGA Tour player who aced two holes in a row during a 1971 tournament
63 Sicily's most famous mountain
64 Calculator precursors
65 Like some basements
66 B.A. and B.S.
67 Looked for gold
68 They should stay on the ball

DOWN

1 Masters or British Open

2 Woman's name that means "peace"
3 Posh snack spots
4 Little helper of Santa
5 Golf great born in Latrobe, Pennsylvania
6 Make ___ for it (bolt)
7 Half: Prefix
8 ___ fault (overly)
9 Tolstoy title word
10 "I'm always the ___ know!"
11 Certain ball position
12 Facial reaction to a made putt
13 Band's output
18 Kind of power
23 "High Hopes" and "Love and Marriage" lyricist
25 Canadian, say

28 Leaf of a fern
29 ___ bounds (whither a duffer's shots)
30 Up to the point when
31 Vucinich of the Senior PGA Tour
32 ___ Lake Golf Club (host of the 2001 U.S. Amateur)
33 Bruce Springsteen tune "___ the One"
34 Follow the recipe's instructions
35 Bright star
36 Like Fuzzy Zoeller
40 Wok, say
41 Funny Foxx
43 Piece of equipment for a greenskeeper
44 "I'll Stand ___"
46 Hjorth and others
47 Pale purple color
50 School assignment
51 Former ABC exec Arledge
52 Makes, as a putt
53 A kid might take it onto a golf course in the winter
54 Tom of the Senior PGA Tour
55 In ___ (stuck)
56 Action film star Jackie
57 Not again
61 ___-Wan Kenobi
62 Ike's initials

ANSWER, PAGE 95

P.S.

One more thing; solve this puzzle.

ACROSS

1 "Take ___ from me ..." (words from the club pro)
5 Sutton of the Tour
8 Sudden contraction
13 Tiger or Jack, for short
15 Leave in amazement
16 East ___ (nation since 2002)
17 Courtroom happening
18 Like some divot-making shots
19 Declares to the world
20 Unfortunate score-padder
23 Solheim Cup team
24 #1
25 Five-time second-leading money winner on the LPGA Tour
30 They go in the fireplace

31 "Xanadu" band
32 "___ it short" (words on the green)
35 Opposite of "neath"
36 One place to buy golf gloves
39 Engage in courtship
40 Upstate New York city
42 Place to wash up
43 Corporate head honchos
44 He won three majors in the last ten years of his life
48 Russian ruler until 1917
49 Hither and ___
50 Pre-shot ritual
56 Weight loss plan ___-Meal
57 "Tin ___"

58 WWII plane ___ Gay
60 Swashbuckling Flynn
61 Former Bush spokesman Fleischer
62 English county that's home to Plymouth and Exeter
63 Long-term military tactic
64 "Hold on a ___!"
65 Cuts down a tree, maybe

DOWN

1 Perform in a play
2 University of Maryland golfer, for short
3 "Would ___ to you?"
4 Brown strip

5 Part of an axe
6 Farthest from the hole
7 "___ serious about this!"
8 Captain Kirk was on one
9 Important
10 Run ___ (go nuts)
11 "___ hear!"
12 Title for the lady of the house
14 Shot from the sand trap
21 Cake portion
22 On the ___ (ready to drive)
25 Frost or Longfellow
26 "Get ___!" (advice to someone who's always losing control during his swing?)
27 ___-mo camera

28 Tournament-running clubs
29 Comparatively fresh
30 Six-time Tour winner Graham
33 Putt measurement
34 Talking-___ (verbal thrashings)
36 Wage range
37 Modest home
38 Does what one's told
41 Mail-order book
43 Sharp-pointed teeth
45 ___ King Cole
46 Author Jong and others
47 Amazed the crowd
50 Prefix with scope or meter
51 Like holes-in-one
52 Relieve of, as the yips
53 Long story
54 Astronomical wonder
55 Eerie light
56 ___ Moines
59 Part of Q&A

50

ANSWER, PAGE 96

HEAVY METAL

Get out your brassie for this one.

ACROSS

1 Sunny city
6 Price revealer
9 Like the name "Calcavecchia": Abbr.
13 Pentium company
14 Solo for opera stars
16 Golf course lament
17 Feature of many clubs
19 Big holders for coffee
20 Place to plop down
21 Chinese meal feature
23 Supreme ending
24 Swing swinger
25 Naomichi ___ Ozaki
26 "What did I say?"
28 Man of the house
29 Second half
34 Rare result for Tiger
37 Club part
38 Place for a sand wedge
39 Each
40 Bus rider's coin
41 It wasn't built in a day
42 Seaweed
43 Greek god of war
44 1960s hit "Walk Away ___"
45 Doing well on the links
47 Gardening tool
48 Title for a lady
49 January in golf
50 Suffix for perfection
53 President on the penny
55 Kevin Costner golf movie
59 ___ the hole (where made putts go)
60 ___ one's time (pass the hours)
62 Tommy Armour's nickname
64 End of list letters

65 ___-day (kind of vitamin)
66 "May ___ your order?"
67 Long fish
68 Big Internet letters
69 Red Sea crosser

DOWN

1 ___ putt (fail to make par, perhaps)
2 Prefix meaning "between"
3 Mr. T's group, with "The"
4 Face in match play
5 "___ give you that one" (gimme offer)
6 Lake between states
7 "I smell ___!"
8 Set of golf clubs, perhaps
9 Letters for debtors
10 Mid-mashie, nowadays
11 Landers and Richards
12 Like many duffers' balls
15 Patronized the clubhouse, maybe
18 Pro ___
22 Set a price of
25 Hole-in-one feeling
27 Main course
28 Dottie of the LPGA Tour
29 1991 British Open champ Ian ___-Finch
30 Par-3 wonders
31 100 yrs.
32 Scorecard factoid
33 Sword used in Olympic competitions
34 Capital of Azerbaijan

35 Tournament type
36 The last golfer to get one at the Olympics was Canada's George Lyon in 1904
37 ___ song (cheaply)
40 ___-in (short putt)
44 George's predecessor
46 Q followers
47 Big name in golf patrons
49 Els rival
50 Pizarro conquered them
51 Tend to the fire
52 Drags around
53 Busy as ___
54 Backspin on the ball
56 Letters seen in personal ads
57 One of Christopher Columbus's ships
58 Queen of the Nile, for short
59 Ratio words
61 African hero
63 Lip of the cup

THAT'S A LIE!

Lies you may face on the links.

ACROSS

1 Golf course concern
7 He lost the 1989 Masters by missing a two-footer
11 Come-___ (marketing ploys)
14 Cezanne work "Boy ___ Vest"
15 Horrifying beast
16 Become decayed
17 She won on five different tours in 1994
18 ___ lie (lie that may not be great)
20 Singer Yoko
21 Measurement for putts
22 Stopping action on a ball
23 Title for a knight
25 Adjective for Daly drives
27 Made points and counterpoints
29 "Now I get it!"
30 Worry
32 Like Jack Nicklaus: Abbr.
33 Omaha's loc.
34 "Where ___?" (ball-searcher's query)
36 Fight off, as a rally attempt
40 Guy's mate
41 ___ lie (lie that may be on the edge of a bunker)
43 Two-time major winner Floyd
44 "You ___ lucky!" (words to a player who gets a fortunate bounce)
46 Cry as one's ball flies into a water hazard
47 Use the wrong club, e.g.
48 Police radio letters
50 Advice from the club pro
52 Cart ___ (golf course charge)
53 Hurts on the schoolyard
57 "A mouse!"
58 Fiori and Dougherty
59 Prefix with potent
60 "The Lion King" sound
62 Tax mo.
64 ___ lie (lie on a slope)
66 Couldn't stop looking
69 The Tiger Woods ___ (1997-?)
70 Send a page to
71 Montana's capital
72 Middle East nat.
73 Vegas numbers
74 Ate away

DOWN

1 Comic Caesar
2 Japanese airline
3 ___ lie (lie for a lucky player)
4 Moran of "Happy Days"
5 Start the hole
6 Unit that holes are measured in: Abbr.
7 Source of many great one-liners about golf
8 Gawked
9 Big divot, slangily
10 "Now, wait just a second!"
11 John Glenn was once in it
12 "48 HRS" actor
13 High-spirited horse
19 Lessen
21 City of central California
23 ___ different tune (changed one's mind)
24 Start of gossip
26 Solo in an opera
28 LPGA Hall of Fame member
31 ___ lie (lie on bare ground or thin grass)
35 Less big
37 ___ lie (lie improved by a player)
38 Dog-___ (like some old books)
39 Harp-like instruments
41 Takes a bounce along the fairway
42 "Uh-uh"
45 Some sheets are made of it
49 ___ lie (lie sometimes called a "fried egg")
51 Kristi Yamaguchi or Tara Lipinski
53 Portends
54 Georgia college
55 1978 Nobel Peace Prize winner Sadat
56 Moved a gondola
61 Site of nine Winter Olympics
63 ___ Alto
65 Cable letters
66 Pronoun for Se Ri Pak or Kelli Kuehne
67 Chemical suffix
68 Tom Morris Senior, to Tom Morris Junior

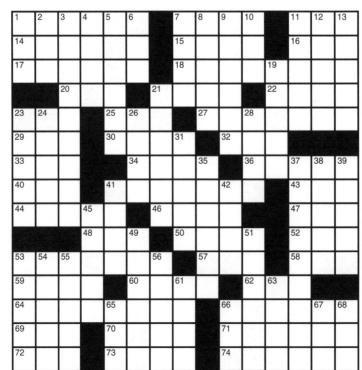

ANSWER, PAGE 83

AUTHOR, AUTHOR!

Who wrote the book on golf?

ACROSS

1 Kind of coffee
5 Greenskeepers cut it
10 Dot on a die
13 She sheep
14 Source of golf news, perhaps
15 Site of the Taj Mahal
16 His golf memoirs are entitled "The Snake in the Sand Trap"
18 Birdies on par threes
19 Mr. Maltbie
20 Claws of eagles
22 "Keep ___!" ("Don't give up!")
24 Actor Billy ___ Williams
26 June honorees
27 Humble homes
29 Yonder objects
31 Not any different
32 Ball ___ (course sight)
35 Fail to sing the words
38 "Big Blue"
39 His golf memoirs are entitled "Confessions of a Hooker"
40 Opening hole number

41 "___ we play through?"
42 "The Sun Also Rises" name
43 Not exactly golf attire
44 See eye to eye
46 Requests of
48 Gait for a horse
49 Striped man on a basketball court
52 Playoff hole necessitators
53 Champagne-and-orange-juice drink
55 Beat after 18 holes
57 Like ___ of bricks
58 Pulitzer-winning author who penned "Golf Dreams"
63 Word in many scores at Carnoustie

64 Neighborhoods
65 Morally wicked
66 To be, to Miguel Angel Jimenez
67 Moves like a putt
68 D.C. party

DOWN

1 1960 British Open champ Nagle
2 Lose a bet on the links, say
3 Word in wedding announcements
4 Sitting on top of
5 Norman on the links
6 Couldn't say enough good things
7 In ___ situation (hitting from behind a tree, maybe)

8 It may be original
9 Chimney sweep covering
10 Humorist who wrote "Golf Without Tears"
11 Cleek and niblick
12 Move ahead of on the scoreboard
15 Book for travelers
17 Pure memorization
21 Love to pieces
22 Addis ___ (Ethiopia's capital)
23 Golf great who wrote the classic instruction manual "How to Play Your Best Golf All the Time"
25 Group characteristics

27 "And just ___ about to swing, a fly starts buzzing around my head ..." (golf course excuse)
28 Reacted to missing a putt, maybe
30 Prefix meaning "seven"
33 "Li'l ___"
34 That woman
36 Volts or meters
37 "Take ___ your leader!"
39 Golfers Yancey and Greene
43 Moved like a topped ball
45 Thuglike enforcers
47 Part of a process
48 Championship
50 Merman or Waters
51 ___ hole (18th)
53 15-Down contents
54 Slightly open
56 Cochran of the PGA Tour
59 Gold: Spanish
60 "___ been had!"
61 LPGA star Mi Hyun ___
62 Ernie who's won many a tourney

ANSWER, PAGE 85

THE OTHER SIDE

Ten percent of us play like these guys.

ACROSS

1 TPC at ___ Bay
6 Sprint rival
9 Cry to an overhit ball
13 Battle site
14 Sign of things to come
15 Very important
16 1963 British Open champ
18 Mineral stuff
19 "Each Dawn ___" (1939 James Cagney film)
20 Half of Rodriguez's name
21 Ending for north or west
22 ___ Aviv
23 He tied for 5th at the 2000 Nissan Open
28 ___ gin fizz (bar order)
30 Noted club maker
31 Letter in some fraternity names
32 State where Tiger lives: Abbr.
34 Free (of)
35 War god, to the Greeks

36 2004 Masters champ
40 Orderly
41 "___ little teapot ..."
42 Didn't get up
43 Golfing Gary from Scotland
44 Org. for swingers?
45 Sheep hassler
48 He finished 4th at the 2000 Nissan Open
53 Steve Case's co.
55 Faces, as a shot
56 Dawn personified
57 Actress Sorvino
58 Mt. statistic
60 How the four golfers featured herein play
63 Blow a lead, say
64 Bk. writer
65 O'Meara's is in Orlando

66 H.S. tests
67 Like some fast-playing courses
68 Tee times, e.g.: Abbr.

DOWN

1 Powerful force
2 Eats away at
3 Send another invoice
4 Number of times Amy Alcott won the U.S. Women's Open
5 Casual no
6 2054, old-style
7 Letter after bee
8 Shoo-___ (easy winners)
9 Dinah of tournaments
10 Leaves the amateur world behind

11 Get better, like Sutton or O'Meara
12 Victorious shout
14 "I would have swinged him, ___ should have swinged me" (Shakespeare quote about an out-of-control golf rivalry?)
17 Play part
21 Course shade provider
23 Unload
24 Estrada of TV fame
25 Some tactically played golf shots
26 T.C. who almost won the 1985 U.S. Open
27 That guy's

29 "What ___?" ("So?")
33 Pal, to Olazabal
34 Big name in electronics
35 Concerning
36 Lima's country
37 Tops in severity
38 Apple product
39 Suburban practice green?
40 Neither/___
44 Some laptops
46 Didn't go for the green
47 Where many golf balls are lost
49 Up-and-down sequences, often
50 Like John Daly
51 Rock star David Lee___
52 Cigarette remnant
54 Loads up, as cargo
57 L-Q connectors
58 African star
59 Hawaii's Mauna ___
60 Boy who lives near St. Andrews
61 Ryder Cup team: Abbr.
62 "Eureka!"

54

ANSWER, PAGE 87

THE FAB FOURSOME

Didn't you know they were golfers?

ACROSS

1 Slow floaters
6 Tour player Beck, and some of his shots
11 David Duval has done them for Charles Schwab
14 Texas building
15 Attacked
16 It's 4½ inches across
17 "Sgt. Pepper's" song about golf course maintenance?
19 ___ tear (playing well)
20 "The Name of the Rose" author Umberto
21 And others: Abbr.
22 LPGA leading money winner, 1978, 1979, and 1985
24 He's not buying it
27 Big name in boxing
28 "Magical Mystery Tour" song Craig Stadler might sing?
35 Airborne distractions
38 Word muttered after a mulligan
39 Opening hole
40 Like the crowd at the 1999 Ryder Cup
41 They come with downs
42 Army leader?
44 Self-centered entity
45 Cookie you might eat at the Nabisco Championship?
46 They go on fishermen's hooks
47 "White Album" song about not letting another group play through?
51 Only three-letter winner of the U.S. Women's Open
52 1970 Masters champ Billy
56 Fighter pilot's button
59 Aoki of the Senior Tour
62 Cry Sergio Garcia loves to hear
63 Deserving
64 "Help!" song about not being intimidated by Davis on the links?
68 "___ give you that" (permission to pick up a gimme)
69 "___ sight!"
70 Agitated
71 "___ the season ..."
72 Retrieve the ball from the cup, perhaps
73 Actress Spacek

DOWN

1 1960 decathlon champ Johnson
2 Miller of the LPGA
3 Brad on the Tour
4 Site of a Penna. nuclear accident
5 Qass, to Vijay Singh
6 Trevino likes to do it with fans while he plays
7 Laughter syllables
8 Tiger, to many
9 Buddy
10 "A Streetcar Named Desire" character
11 "There's never ___ around when you need one!"
12 Beach hill
13 Uncool type
18 Cold cause
23 Baby ___
25 Requiring a playoff
26 Like two-foot putts
27 Sympathetic sounds
29 Senior and Buy.com
30 Famed golf supporter Bob and others
31 ___ salts
32 Rice-a-___
33 Watt or ohm
34 Gets a look at
35 Couples who can play golf well?
36 The PGA's features a swinging golfer
37 Victor's statement
42 Swedish supergroup of pop music
43 Four-time major champ Floyd and namesakes
45 Wood you might hit on a bad drive?
48 Acorn, eventually
49 Barbecue locales, often
50 Environmentalist's college major: Abbr.
53 Office betting setups
54 Santa's crew
55 Thin and frail
56 Work at a paper, perhaps
57 Linkster Inkster
58 Long fish
59 Comparative words
60 Explorer Hernando de ___
61 Take ___ (snooze)
65 Pharaoh King ___
66 Many mos.
67 52, to Caesar

IN LAST PLACE

Players used to it, in a way.

ACROSS

1 Green flapper
5 Unfavorable, as a lie
8 Healthy places
12 Downhill from, as the pin
14 Suffix meaning "state or condition"
16 Give pointers to
17 ___-American (Mark Calcavecchia, for instance)
18 Solemn pledge
19 Scat singer Fitzgerald
20 Two-time major winner known for playing very quickly
23 Good place to be on the leader board
26 One of Jack's biggest rivals
27 Richie who sang "La Bamba"
28 "Slammin' Sammy" and family
30 Country club fees
32 Mao ___-tung
33 He won $536,146 on the 1999 Senior PGA Tour
36 Explorer Hernando de ___
37 Light switch settings
38 Quaint adjective for a "shoppe"
42 Three-time U.S. Women's Open winner who also won a gold medal in the javelin throw at the 1932 Summer Olympics

47 Spot on a die
50 "That ___ great shot!"
51 Lost-ball searcher's cry
52 Prince Albert's location
54 2nd-place finisher at the 2000 Mercedes Championships
55 ___ Today
56 He won $195,571 on the 1999 Senior PGA Tour
60 Clarinet cousin
61 North who's only won three PGA Tour events ... but two of them were U.S. Opens
62 Feared mammal on the links
66 Bathroom floor piece

67 "I'm gonna have to lay ___" (course comment)
68 68 is an excellent one
69 Pace
70 The Presidents Cup mo.
71 Like some fast greens

DOWN

1 Agt. Mulder's employer
2 ___ another group play through
3 State where two-time PGA Championship winner Larry Nelson was born: Abbr.
4 "A good walk spoiled," in Mark Twain's famous quote

5 Nineteenth hole purchase, perhaps
6 Have ___ in (influence)
7 Brainless one, slangily
8 ___ Houston Open
9 Little ball of food, as for animals
10 Senior PGA Tour player Doyle and namesakes
11 Not crowded
13 "How ___ do that?"
15 Scoop the ball, as with a wedge
21 Exuberance
22 Effortlessness
23 Reproachful sounds
24 ___'clock (lunch break end)

25 Full of bounce
29 ___ scene (very crowded)
30 Tony of "Taxi"
31 ___ Major (Great Bear constellation)
34 Baird and Caldwell
35 Yesteryear
39 In ___ of (replacing)
40 Speaker's platform
41 "¿Cómo ___ usted?" (greeting at Valderrama)
43 Set to putt first
44 Japanese war cry
45 It might keep your ball rolling
46 Stocks, bonds, cars, and golf clubs
47 Some Delta employees
48 Soon
49 Con's out, sometimes
53 Move stealthily
54 Country where you can play the Mena House Golf Course at the foot of the pyramids
57 Preposition before "the rough"
58 Schooling: Abbr.
59 Beem of the Tour
63 ___ long way (last)
64 Blunder
65 Like a golfer's face after shanking one into the water

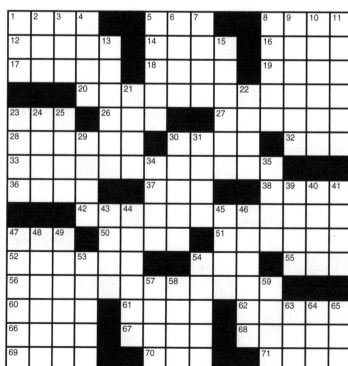

56

ANSWER, PAGE 91

V-J DAY

Singhing a player's praises.

ACROSS

1 Language in which "Vijay" means "victory"
6 Vijay Singh's island home
10 Green guarder
14 Shaquille or Tatum
15 Little bills
16 ___ close second (barely trail)
17 Tour honor won by Vijay in 1993
20 Motel
21 This, in Havana
22 Diplomatic bldg.
23 Verve
25 Hairdo type
27 1957 U.S. Open winner Dick ___
31 Golfers toss grass to check it
33 "Give ___ rest!"
35 Org. that rescues motorists
36 Big trucks
39 Card game with a special deck
40 Play sections
41 Vijay won it in 1998

45 Horrendous creature
46 Home: Abbr.
47 The yips affect them
48 You: French
49 ___ Byron Nelson Classic
50 Actress Teri of "Tootsie"
52 Rough surprise, maybe
54 "___ bien!"
56 Mozart's "___ kleine Nachtmusik"
60 "That's ___ brainer"
62 Symbol of servitude
64 Go to waste
65 Florida city where Vijay lives with his wife and son
70 Utterance following "Fore!"?

71 "Break ___!"
72 Take to the tub
73 British star Jacklin
74 Old money in Milan
75 Club metal

DOWN

1 Not vert.
2 Hole-___
3 Some bright signs
4 S. ___ (Nebr. neighbor)
5 "Would ___ to you?"
6 Paid, as the bill
7 Deserving and about to get
8 Boeing product
9 "Who ___ kidding?"
10 Ted on the Tour
11 Have regrets about

12 Santa ___, California
13 Golfers like to save it
18 Network that broadcasts a lot of golf
19 Jane Austen classic
24 Number of times Payne Stewart won on the 1999 PGA Tour
26 Small
28 Comfy cruiser
29 Mother's dinnertime command
30 Grates harshly
32 Ending meaning "kind of"
34 "___ bad!"
36 Dalmatian features
37 Encourage
38 Jose ___ Olazabal

39 Great times
40 "It's ___ thing!"
42 1959 Masters champ ___ Wall, Jr.
43 Go head-to-head
44 Informative airwaves letters
49 Littler or Sarazen
50 Archer or Burns
51 "___ silly question ..."
53 Legendary Whitworth
55 Cup of golf
57 More than merely mad
58 Night, in Nicaragua
59 Merman or Waters
61 Shape of some greens
63 Wanes
65 ___ away (seal, as a victory)
66 Cry of discovery
67 "Smoking or ___?"
68 Inventor Whitney
69 Absorb, as losses

ANSWER, PAGE 93

TO THE LETTER

B a good sport and C if you can solve this.

ACROSS

1 Clumsy fool
5 Topeka's place
11 Day two of most PGA Tour events: Abbr.
14 Lhasa ___ (breed of dog)
15 Most unfeeling, as a stare
16 ___ Abner
17 I
20 Finish with
21 Film director Craven
22 Modern golfer's distractions
23 Army outposts: Abbr.
25 Dachshund or Doberman
26 Y
34 Bathroom, to Nick Faldo
35 Having a scent
36 Military group
38 Shares a border with
40 State that's home to the Bethany Bay Golf Club: Abbr.
41 Get in the way of a shot, as a tree might
42 "Fuggedaboudit!"
43 Where Dan Quayle once served
45 Two-time PGA Championship winner Diegel
46 J
49 Top or yo-yo
50 In the style of
51 Tour player Fulton
54 ___-Locka, Florida
57 "I believe ___!"
61 T
64 Actress Gardner
65 Stopped the day's play, maybe
66 Black-and-white treat
67 Money for Ayako Okamoto
68 1998 was a very good year for him
69 Loch ___ Monster

DOWN

1 Feature of some tough holes
2 Kemper ___
3 Like some golf clubs or cars
4 Fill the gas tank to the brim
5 First aid ___
6 "Don't have ___, man!" (Bart Simpson line)
7 Front or back
8 Groups of golf clubs
9 Wood used in making woods
10 Every ___ the way (all along)
11 Pin attachment
12 Stir up
13 Bad things
18 Musical beginnings
19 Amount of groceries
24 Lay down earth
25 Flop of a firecracker
26 St. Andrews family
27 Programmable worker
28 "There ___!" (encouraging words)
29 Onetime Tiger dater Tyra Banks, for example
30 Sphere of conflict
31 Halt in play
32 WWII plane ___ Gay
33 ___-Roni
37 Some boxing wins: Abbr.
39 Talked up
41 European city where you can play at the Golf Club Wannsee
43 Engage in espionage
44 Meal at the British Open
47 Argentine golfer Eduardo ___
48 Refuse to give in
51 Further from the hole
52 Major winner of 1997
53 Money from the bank
54 Ron Howard role
55 Former Clinton cabinet member Federico
56 Suffix for teen
58 Days gone by
59 "Bravo!" relatives
60 Scary saucers
62 Where John McCain fought, for short
63 Neighbor of Mont.

ANSWER, PAGE 95

WHICH WAY TO GO?

Just follow the directions.

ACROSS

1 Intentional hook
5 See 65-Across
9 Beth Daniel or Fred Couples, astrologically
14 Zippo
15 ___ difficult lie (might be in trouble)
16 Approximating word
17 U.S. Open winner, 1978 and 1985
19 Actress Winger
20 Neither here ___ there (like a duffer's lost ball?)
21 Crowd reaction to a ball in the water
23 Greenish blue
24 Less refined
27 Finishing the back nine
29 Cold one
30 Mined stuff
31 Robe holder
35 David on the Tour
37 Network that often airs golf
38 First name in African golf
40 You'd like to hole it out
43 Army beds
45 Mike "Fluff" Cowan, notably
47 Putting first
48 Milk go-withs
50 Longed (for)
52 ___-iron
53 Occasion for the National Guard
55 NBA Hall of Famer Archibald
56 Have
57 Tour player Forsman
59 Word in many California city names
61 ___ break for it (ran)
63 "... and all ___ was this lousy T-shirt"
65 With 5-Across, 1986 PGA Tour Player of the Year
67 The sun
68 Steam
70 ___ Classic
75 "A Night at the ___"
76 See 4-Down
77 The Golden Bear's state
78 CIA Director George
79 Give off
80 "Hey, buddy!"

DOWN

1 Double-helix material
2 Skittered along, as a golf ball
3 Tally one's scorecard
4 With 76-Across, 1990 PGA Tour Player of the Year
5 God with a magic hammer
6 "The ___ on the Shore" (1991 Ryder Cup nickname)
7 Concerning
8 Jerry Yang's internet company
9 Carnoustie boy
10 Sarcastic agreement
11 Texas-based Senior PGA Tour player
12 In the country
13 "___ of Two Cities"
18 Like 5-Down
22 Modest home
24 Tour star Mediate
25 Ann ___, Michigan
26 Cialis ___
28 Defeat
32 Chip shot's trajectory, ideally
33 End, as a losing streak
34 Used for concealment purposes
36 Actress Farrow
39 Bart Simpson's teacher ___ Krabappel
41 "___ play through?"
42 Laughing beast
44 "___ Married an Axe Murderer" (1993 comedy)
46 Up to now
49 Plea from the sea
51 Introductory versions
54 You might pick it up at the nineteenth hole
57 Earth you should replace
58 Open-mouthed
60 High-minded
62 Throw for ___ (frazzle)
64 Zoomed
66 Rich who won the 1999 Kemper Open
67 Little opening
69 He tells the fuzz
71 VII times VIII
72 Syllables of hesitation
73 "___ the season ..."
74 On a winning streak

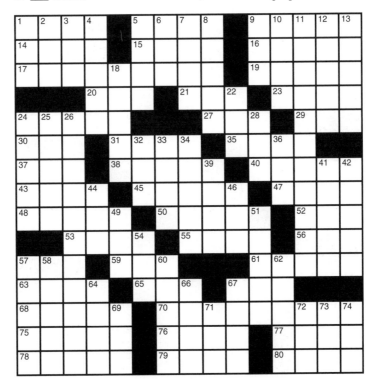

ANSWER, PAGE 96

IT'S IN THE BAG!

A trio in disguise.

ACROSS

1 ___ Open
7 City rumbler
10 Little bit
13 Use an aphrodisiac
14 Clean, as a golf ball
15 Really impress
16 Take advice
17 Competitive advantage
18 Puppy's doc
19 Superlative ending
20 "Tonight Show" announcer Hall
22 Arnie's and others
24 Come into prominence, as a rising star might
27 Like shots over water
28 Church point
31 Mailed, as a contest entry
33 Verb associated with Mark McCormack
35 ___ hot streak (playing well)
36 Tenn. city
40 Nat. dissolved in 1991
41 1960 decathlon champ Johnson
43 "Would ___ to you?" (golfer's reply to "did you really shoot a 75?")
44 "Let's ___ the fifteenth" (golf announcer's sentence)
45 Trajectory
46 Tabloid contents
48 ___ ante (makes things more interesting)
51 Ford bomb
52 Stadium cousin
55 Tom Kite, as of 2000
57 First name of three U.S. Women's Open champs— Spuzich, Haynie, and Palmer
59 Fiori and namesakes
60 Red ___ (debt)
63 Like Ross Perot's 1992 pres. candidacy
64 Grooves in the road
66 Puts a tax on
69 Historically
70 Singer Brickell
71 TPC at ___ (course in Potomac, Maryland)
72 ___ Caledonia
73 Commotion
74 Just

DOWN

1 ___ Kan (pet food company)
2 One of five greats
3 It may provide a soft lie for your ball
4 Dawdle
5 Last three letters of many languages
6 1966 hit "Walk Away ___"
7 Like putts when you've got the yips
8 "Rules of Golf" org.
9 Two-time winner on the 1999 Ladies' Tour Steinhauer
10 Love on the links?
11 "Eight Days ___" (Beatles tune)
12 King of the golf course?
14 The French serve it with a baguette
21 Ruth and J
23 Actress nominated for an Oscar for "Good Will Hunting"
25 Ladies' Tour player Mallon
26 Feminine suffix
28 More than self-confident
29 El ___, Texas
30 Part of MIT
32 Puts down a road
34 Paleozoic and others
37 Sigh of resignation
38 Club ___
39 Part of a golf club
42 They may be fine
47 1928 and 1929 PGA Championship winner Diegel
49 Got the standard score
50 Wind up
52 Thai, e.g.
53 Place to practice driving
54 Give money to the ol' alma mater
56 Koran reader's faith
58 Mercedes rival
61 Number of holes on some courses
62 Boat's balance
65 "___ Cup" (1996 Kevin Costner golf movie)
67 Night before
68 Tough to trick

ANSWER, PAGE 81

SOUNDS LIKE A GOLFER

Weir hoping you'll like this one.

ACROSS

1 Lhasa ___ (shaggy breed of dog)
5 Georgia ___ (David Duval's alma mater)
9 ___ Senior Open
12 ___ 1-wood (drives)
14 Some razors
16 Pie ___ mode
17 Stewart, the golfer who loves to cook?
19 Part of Ryder Cup victory celebrations
20 Big Internet initials
21 Ice cream rival of Ben & Jerry
22 Darren Clarke's country: Abbr.
23 Karrie, the international golfer?
28 "___ you!"
29 Bambi, e.g.
30 Symbol of Aries
31 Hit the links
33 Funny, funny guy
35 Winemakers Martini and ___
39 Set a price

41 Noted nucleic acid
42 ___ a stroke (bogeys)
43 Beast with a horn on its snout
44 Like some circumstances
46 Chinese money
47 Golfer Scherrer
49 Have-___ (poor folk)
51 ___-cone
52 A few strokes up on Se Ri?
56 "Give ___ break!"
57 "Without further ___ ..."
58 Teachers' org.
59 High-protein breakfast food
60 John's sets of back-to-back victories?
66 Guy's date

67 Tournament locales
68 Mulligan, maybe
69 It has a frothy head
70 Take some time off
71 Unpleasantness for the nose

DOWN

1 Black and white sea bird
2 Beatles song "___ Love You"
3 Golf bag contents
4 Adam Sandler did not win one for "Happy Gilmore"
5 Evidence of time on the links, perhaps
6 Letters meaning "and so on"

7 Reacted badly to losing
8 Left-___ (Mickelson, for example)
9 Sir, in India
10 Book jacket quote
11 Zoo structure
13 Grab ___ of (seize)
15 Direction of a lofty shot
18 Lee of the Senior PGA Tour
23 Like Ian Woosnam
24 Jumbo or Joe
25 Bizarre
26 Favorite household chore of golfers?
27 Atlanta campus
28 Practice boxing
32 Busybody
34 Spooky deck of cards

36 "Stars and Stripes Forever" composer
37 Punish a child corporally
38 "Ignorance of the law ___ excuse"
40 Thingamajigs
45 Prefix for centric
48 Where the ball is when some golfers curse
50 "Come back and ___ again real soon!"
52 Unlike using your shoe to improve your lie
53 It'll move you up a couple of strokes
54 Actor Nick of "48 HRS"
55 Casals or Picasso
56 Huge
61 Exultant utterance
62 Sunshine-saving clock setting: Abbr.
63 Tupperware topper
64 "The Name of the Rose" writer
65 To be, to Sergio Garcia

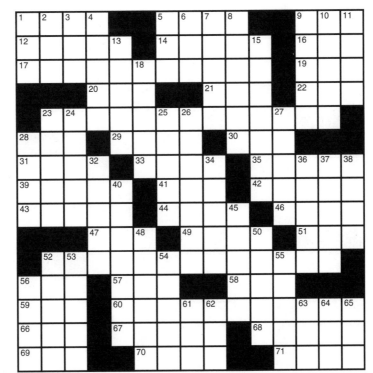

ANSWER, PAGE 83

IN MEMORIAM

Remembering Payne Stewart.

ACROSS

1 Make, as a score on the links
6 Tour player Chris
11 Rebukes to loud fans
14 African city home to the Gezira Sporting Club golf course
15 Find ___ for the common cold
16 Element with the shortest name
17 Payne Stewart, at SMU
19 Lennon's lady
20 King, to Sergio Garcia
21 One-iron, old-style
22 Doggie name
23 Pas' mates
24 Payne participated in it five times
27 On ___ (ready to drive)
30 It may climb a clubhouse wall
31 Carnoustie terrain
32 Like Tiger's paychecks
35 He's busy in Apr.

38 Payne won it in 1989
42 White or Red
43 Start
44 ___-up (suppressed)
45 January on the links
46 Playing hooky, maybe
49 Payne's signature pants
54 Eighteenth hole, say
55 Fairway feature, sometimes
56 Less than ninety degrees
58 Cotton gin inventor Whitney
61 Madison or Fifth: Abbr.
62 Payne's signature hat
65 1964 U.S. Open winner Venturi

66 More than like
67 1969 and 1970 U.S. Women's Open winner Caponi
68 Neither Rep. nor Dem.
69 Rosie of the Women's Tour
70 Average drive distance, number of birdies in a season, etc.

DOWN

1 Hurt permanently
2 Irwin of the Senior Tour
3 Slick
4 "Are you a man ___ mouse?"
5 He meows
6 Like holes-in-one
7 Comparatively chilly

8 What you must be to score a hole-in-one
9 Time period
10 Money for Ayako Okamoto
11 Unemotional
12 Vijay Singh, for example
13 Look where one shouldn't
18 "What ___ is new?"
22 Work at the golf shop snack bar, maybe
23 Thermometer contents: Abbr.
25 I say, in Venezuela
26 At par
27 Not for here
28 The Loch Ness monster, probably
29 Course shaders
31 Army cops, for short

33 Imitate
34 The Beatles' "Lovely ___"
35 1985 U.S. Open sensation
36 Beer amount
37 Fitting
39 Slice counterpart
40 Women's star ___-Marie Palli
41 Went too fast in the golf cart
45 650, to Romans
47 Tour star Daniel
48 Family of "Slammin' Sammy"
49 Color of Payne's 49-Across, often
50 1958 Best Actor winner David
51 "Can ___ you a hand?"
52 Baseball's ___ Martinez
53 One over, maybe
57 Takes advantage of
58 Sicily's Mt. ___
59 Ash Wednesday to Easter
60 Golden years funds
62 ___ Mahal
63 Shakespearean fuss
64 "Do ___ Enter"

ANSWER, PAGE 85

THE WINNERS' CIRCLE

Four from a select group.

ACROSS

1 Hole markers
5 Pro shop purchase, maybe
10 Tour player Andy
14 Prison, in England
15 Singer Lena
16 "___ You"
17 WINNER, 1995 AND 1996
20 Apiece
21 Simon & Garfunkel's "I ___ Rock"
22 Spooky ability
23 WINNER, 1989 AND 1990
28 Major winner of 1978 and 1985
30 Houston's pro hockey team
31 Finds, as the green
33 Cleek or mashie
34 Kite, Watson, or Lehman
35 Final scores
39 Uncle, to Olazabal
40 WINNER, 1998
42 Lemon meringue or apple
43 One of the tours

45 Neither here ___ there
46 Without penalty, like gimmes and mulligans
47 Jack Nicklaus associate Larry ___
49 French-speaking Caribbean country
50 State that's home to the Kennebec Heights Golf Club
53 WINNER, 1991
55 Play a part
56 Knock (on)
58 Avian symbol of wisdom
59 WHAT THEY WON
66 Naval rank: Abbr.
67 Els of South Africa

68 Word of warning
69 Where M.D.'s and R.N.'s work
70 Emotionless, as a stare
71 Like some greens

DOWN

1 Tour group
2 First name of two 1991 major winners
3 ___-playing team captain
4 Falls victim to, as a banana peel
5 Greg Norman's nickname
6 Santa's syllables
7 Conquistador's quest
8 Make mad
9 Give the appearance of
10 Jackson and Diddley

11 Participate in the tournament
12 As ___ resort
13 Beautiful young woman
18 Golf cart starters
19 "___ of the North"
23 Fisherman's needs
24 Really weird
25 Site of a 1997 Justin Leonard win
26 Composer Stravinsky
27 Candidate for an award
29 Province where the Bell Canadian Open is often held: Abbr.
32 Tiger Woods or David Duval
34 Part of a country: Abbr.

36 Masters month
37 Lose the trust of, maybe
38 "What did I ever ___ him?"
40 ___ up (recovers from a night on the town)
41 Early video game
44 "Am ___ the green?"
46 Hit a slump
48 Daiwa golf clubs, for instance
49 Laughter sounds
50 ___ play competition
51 Sound that may distract a golfer
52 Hot couples
54 Ryder Cup issue
57 Blows away
60 Ref
61 L-P connectors
62 A, to Bernhard Langer
63 Senator or congressman, slangily
64 Historical time period
65 Driving range barrier

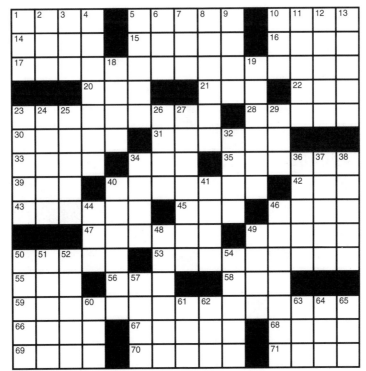

ANSWER, PAGE 87

BORN TO GOLF

It's all in their names.

ACROSS

1 Bob who loved golf
5 PGA Championship, for example
10 In the area
14 Spoken
15 Worthy of ridicule
16 Use as a reference
17 Three-time Masters winner (and what he is)
19 Got better, like cheddar
20 Noted golf tournament sponsoring company
21 Sutton and others
22 Home to Brigham Willows golf course
24 Just on the market
25 Rock star Brian
26 LPGA Tour player Leigh ___ Mills
27 Good place to be on the leader board
30 Strokes behind
32 Woman, un-P.C.-style
34 Ryder Cup winner, sometimes

36 Santa's syllables
38 Spooky Serling
40 The Abominable Snowman
41 She won $178,128 on the 1999 LPGA Tour (and where she putts)
44 College golf star, maybe: Abbr.
46 Big pot for coffee
47 Nine-digit identifier: Abbr.
48 Golf course, slangily
50 It rows your boat
52 Optional transport on 48-Across
55 Take a swing
56 Director Howard
58 Ending for mountain or auction

60 Time in history
62 Meat cut
64 Senior player Aoki
65 Golfer's headgear
66 Like some pin placements
68 Good pal of Mark O'Meara (and some of his clubs)
71 "Woe ___!"
72 "Let's Make ___"
73 For nothing
74 Educator with a list
75 Two-time U.S. Women's Open winner Sheehan
76 Tallies up one's score

DOWN

1 He won four U.S. Opens in six years
2 Gave a speech

3 Like many miniature golf holes
4 Actor Ron who played Tarzan on TV
5 Northern Italian metropolis
6 Watch variety
7 Haas and Delsing
8 Hole-in-___
9 Show the show again
10 Org. 44-Across plays under
11 Course number
12 Had ham
13 Stripe color on some golf balls
18 Prodigy, for short
23 Explosive trio of letters
26 Sleep like ___
28 ___ of bounds (hook result, maybe)

29 Greek letter
31 Sound made by a John Daly drive
33 Indoor sport site
35 Laughing beast
37 Payne Stewart's alma mater
39 They once took the MCATs
41 British Open winner, 1964
42 Club choice
43 ___ account
44 Diner order
45 Russia's space station
49 ___ Lanka
51 Do an usher's job
53 Nicklaus's six Masters titles, e.g.
54 Played the stock market
57 In reserve
59 ___ leader (golfer the others try to catch)
61 Church sections
63 Kemper ___
64 "Can ___ you anything?"
66 Executed
67 Suffix for Senegal or Siam
69 Ore. neighbor
70 "Son ___ gun!"

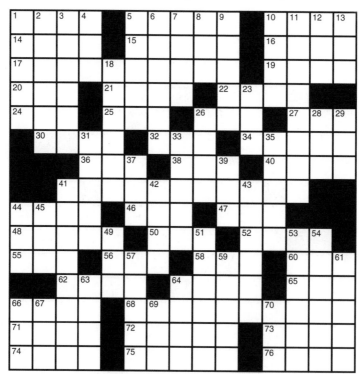

ANSWER, PAGE 89

THE HOLE TRUTH

A humorous quip about keeping score.

ACROSS

1 Basketball start
7 Listening devices
11 Medicine man, for short
14 Winner of two majors in '98
15 "There oughta be ___ against that!"
16 Sky sighting
17 Start of a quip
19 Golf cart path material
20 Picnic problem
21 Not after
22 Friend of Alfalfa and Buckwheat
24 Quip, part 2
28 Kultida Woods, to Tiger
31 Top of the line
32 '70s hairstyles
33 Deal (with)
35 Quip, part 3
39 Mai ___ (cocktail)
40 Fans
43 Second Amendment gp.
44 Speaker of the quip, for short
46 Holes-in-one
47 Forgo dining out
49 Scandinavian capital
51 Penalty ___ (links headache)
52 Quip, part 4
57 Hertz rival
58 Tic-tac-toe victory
59 Advisable tactics
62 Man, to Caesar
63 End of the quip
68 "___ seen it all!"
69 World's Fair word
70 One of the Brady girls
71 Actor Beatty
72 God, to Jean Van de Velde
73 CIA activity

DOWN

1 Party wear, sometimes
2 "___ your side!"
3 Hit hard, as with a golf ball
4 Big galoot
5 Day two of most tournaments: Abbr.
6 Like players who play through
7 Short par 5 goal, perhaps
8 Chicken ___ king
9 Noted brand of golf clubs
10 Jesper Parnevik's country
11 See 60-Down
12 "___ the lowdown, dirty tricks!"
13 ___ Springs, Florida
18 Nine-iron shots get a lot of it
23 Cain slew him
24 Reporter's question
25 "For ___ jolly good ..."
26 Prepares a delayed broadcast
27 Farmer, at times
28 ___ Hari
29 The end ___ era
30 Foursome minus one
33 Wintertime drink
34 Neighbor of Ida.
36 Fascinated by
37 Actor Estrada of "CHiPs"
38 Not nuts
41 Big golfer known for big drives
42 Adam's third son
45 "Cheers" cry
48 "These Guys ___ Good!"
50 Like some greens
51 Play enders
52 1995 U.S. Open winner
53 Mediterranean snack
54 Moved a rowboat
55 "Oh, ___ don't!"
56 The buck stops here?
59 Prefix with liter or meter
60 With 11-Down, 1934 U.S. Open winner
61 Smelting stuff
64 61, in Roman numerals
65 Go ___ (flip out)
66 Drain, as of energy
67 Like Chi Chi Rodriguez's sense of humor

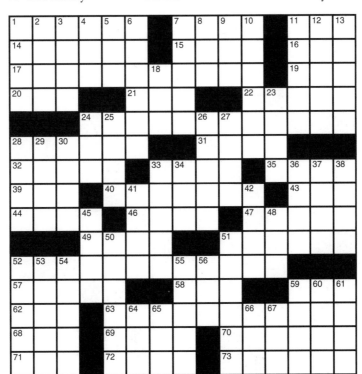

ANSWER, PAGE 91

SWINGING STARS

A little links alliteration.

ACROSS

1 Pebble Beach National ___
6 Lawyer: Abbr.
9 Outer limit, as of the green
13 Place for driving practice
14 ___ Grande River
15 Hot streaks
16 U.S. Women's Open champ of 1980
18 Santa's helpers
19 1951 British Open winner Faulkner
20 Not for keeps
22 Suffix with Manhattan
23 He lost the playoff to Tiger Woods in the 2000 Mercedes Championship
25 Golfing Quayle
26 1940 U.S. Open champion ___ Little
29 Cushion of strokes
31 Come up
32 Tee ___
35 Not real bright

38 Creme ___ creme (elite)
39 Writer who called golf "a good walk spoiled"
40 With more bogeys than birdies
41 Winner of two majors in the '90s
42 Wood and Reagan
43 Shipping container
44 "That makes sense"
46 Everything
47 Nineteenth hole drink
49 Three-time Masters champ
53 ___ Jones
54 Costantino Rocca's land, to him
55 Name a price

58 Actor Jeremy with a golfy surname
60 Two-time winner on the 1999 LPGA Tour
63 "Count ___!"
64 Imitate
65 Winner of back-to-back Masters
66 Plays the eighteenth
67 Letters on Mark McGwire's cap
68 Chubby Checker's dance

DOWN

1 Baby carriage, in England
2 "___ Lama Ding Dong"
3 Semiprecious stone
4 Turkish bigwig
5 Director Brooks

6 Rice-___
7 Championship
8 From head ___ (completely)
9 Electric ___
10 2001 British Open winner
11 Garbo of Hollywood
12 German industrial city
15 Like the atmosphere during a playoff hole
17 State that's home to the Hartford Golf Club: Abbr.
21 Four-time winner on the 1999 Senior PGA Tour ___ Doyle
23 George Will works
24 Wade opponent
26 Cheryl or Alan

27 General vicinity
28 Tour player who won the 1977 U.S. Junior
30 Loved a bunch
32 Wood choice
33 Welsh star Woosnam
34 Prefix with hit
36 "Take ___ your leader!"
37 Pitcher Saberhagen
39 Pay for the round
43 Half a dance
45 It is, to Bernhard Langer
46 Ryder Cup group
47 Stop on ___
48 Actress Sophia
50 Women of the house
51 Caught a few Z's
52 Race car driver Mansell
55 "___ Need Is a Miracle"
56 Lays down earth
57 Granny or half-hitch
59 Greek consonants
61 Fore's counterpart, on a ship
62 Rehnquist's field

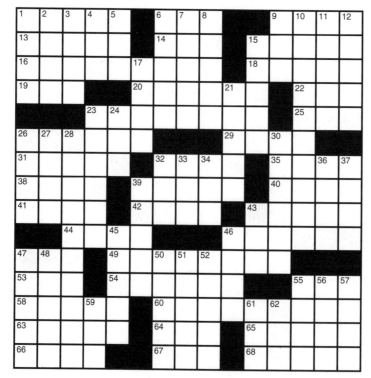

ANSWER, PAGE 93

GOLF IS A FUNNY GAME

And Hollywood agrees.

ACROSS

1 Torrey ___ Country Club
6 The Golden Bear
10 ___ Valley, California
14 Integra makers
15 PGA Tour player Bratton
16 To some small degree
17 1952 Katharine Hepburn/Spencer Tracy movie
19 Have the nerve
20 Creature that could fit on a tee
21 Berlin "the"
22 In a creepy way
24 Cobb and Armstrong
26 It may hold coffee
28 Men
29 1996 Adam Sandler movie
35 Garcia's goodbye
38 Ryan or Mallon
39 Louis XIV, for example
40 Rosters
43 Five-time British Open champ Peter
46 Que. neighbor
47 Slope, as a green

49 Secluded spots
50 Theme of this puzzle
55 Give a hand to
56 Astronaut Grissom
57 Hat worn in 53-Down
60 1996 Kevin Costner movie
63 Forty winks
65 ___ Palmas
67 Course feature golfers avoid
68 1980 Chevy Chase movie
71 School bus driver on "The Simpsons"
72 Gen. Robert ___
73 Snack for Akiko Fukushima
74 Gloom's partner
75 Where you'll find the Fioranello Golf Club

76 Grand ___ National Park, Wyoming

DOWN

1 6-Across, to Gary Nicklaus
2 "___ believe it!"
3 Wacko
4 Baseball stat
5 ___ wedge
6 Makes clogged
7 He knocked out Foreman
8 Birthday party food
9 Like very rough rough
10 More than a mean streak
11 Nat. of 75-Across
12 1963 U.S. Women's Open winner Mills
13 Chemistry suffix

18 Like some slow greens
23 Cath. or Prot., e.g.
25 Golf ___
27 Where Tiger works out
30 Coll. attended by Danielle Ammaccapane
31 ___ up and down (pitch and one-putt)
32 About
33 Powerful chess piece
34 First number to Langer
35 Sleep like ___
36 Fred Flintstone's pet
37 Like Europe's Ryder Cup team: Abbr.
41 TV worker
42 Total

44 Number of times Fuzzy Zoeller won the Masters
45 The majority
48 Like below-par golf scores: Abbr.
51 Crowds at a golf tournament, collectively
52 The president, to military personnel: Abbr.
53 City 10 miles NW from St. Andrews
54 "What can ___?"
58 As ___ resort (in desperation)
59 Overly masculine
60 Noted nonhuman Kansan
61 "___ the Woods" (Broadway play about a duffer's game?)
62 ___ Alto, California
64 "Hey, you!"
66 Won hole(s), at a certain golf competition
67 Pea's place
69 Rep. rival
70 Color

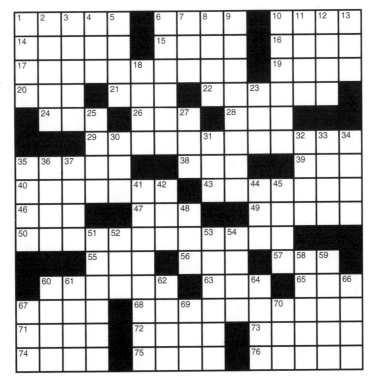

AVOIDING THE BOGEYMAN

Only pleasant results appear herein.

ACROSS

1 Norman of the links
5 Become droopy
8 Some spreads
12 Replay
13 Gambling mecca
14 More achy, as after a long round
15 Ireland, poetically
16 North or Bean
17 Coin choice
18 One of 52
21 "___ tree falls in the woods ..."
22 Holiday ___
23 Steve Miller song used in U.S. Postal Service ads
31 Gets outta Dodge
32 Ball placements
33 Luthor of the comics
34 A bunch
35 Animal hideouts

37 ___ par (sink a long putt, maybe)
38 "Are you a man ___ mouse?"
39 Diplomacy
40 Ebb and high
41 Picture-taker's request
45 "We ___ Family"
46 ___-putt
47 Outstanding beyond compare
54 The Pine Tree State
55 "M*A*S*H" star
56 Symphony players: Abbr.
58 Mt. Aconcagua's range
59 It may be beautiful at Pebble Beach
60 Resort island
61 Creature sometimes seen on golf courses

62 Body part associated with Van Gogh
63 Door opener

DOWN

1 Co. that merged into Verizon
2 ___ avis
3 Like some struggles
4 Golf legend Sarazen
5 "Where the Wild Things Are" author Maurice
6 "The King ___"
7 "The Naked Maja" painter
8 Kool & the Gang hit
9 Saharan
10 Gibson and Blanc
11 Members of a certain tour: Abbr.

13 Children's singer with a one-word name
14 Jagger's group
19 Olive and vegetable
20 Coal region workplaces
23 Plants
24 Allow to attack
25 Exultant cry after a great putt
26 Woods, Duval, Parnevik, etc.
27 Loft
28 "I'm ___ asked!"
29 Flood stopper
30 Former flames
31 Run smoothly
35 What some gloves are made of
36 German's exclamation
37 Comedian Caesar
39 Good scores on par fours

40 Shot hindrance, sometimes
42 LPGA leading money winner, 1974, 1982, and 1983
43 More daring, as a shot over water
44 Marriage acquisition
47 Stewart's favorite part of a window?
48 Caddy, for example
49 Totally collapse under pressure
50 "On the Waterfront" director Kazan
51 Recess of a room
52 Prefix in many fruit drink names
53 Canyon sound
54 Like people who miss three-foot putts
57 Center of a wheel

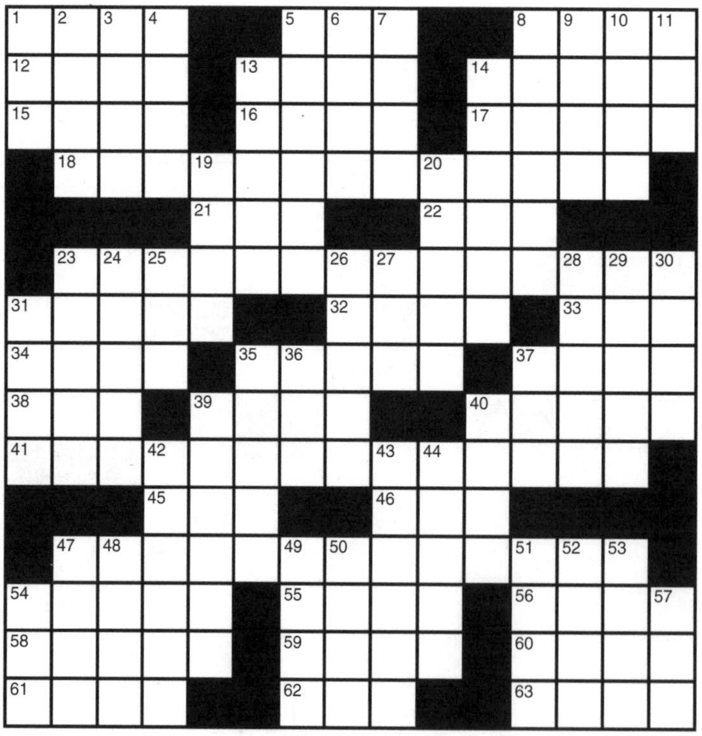

ANSWER, PAGE 96

THE TERRAIN GAME

The places a pitch can land.

ACROSS

1 Tway of the PGA Tour
4 ___-American (Calvin Peete, for example)
8 "Is it bigger ___ breadbox?"
13 "The Simpsons" character
14 Place the ball after hitting it into the water
15 Finds the hole
16 Card player's cry
17 Catching equipment
18 Golf course setting, often
19 Signs, as a contract
21 Spectating no-no
23 Rival
24 ___ off (using a 1-wood, perhaps)
26 Take too many mulligans
29 James Dean's image
31 Pitch, like Tiger does Nike
35 "Zip-A-Dee-Doo-___"

37 "Two guys walk into ___ ..." (joke start)
39 Bill Murray's book "Cinderella Story: My Life in Golf," for instance
40 Opera solo
42 With an ___ (intending on)
44 Performed
45 Byron ___ Classic
47 Zinging Azinger
49 Prefix meaning "earth"
50 Contact lens solutions
52 Grind, as one's teeth
54 Living room pieces
56 Strong finishes on the tour

59 Advisable tactics
62 Beginning for mural or party
64 Part of a golf cart
65 Bring from abroad
68 Tournament stopper
70 ___ Jones (big name on Wall Street)
71 They might keep you up all night
72 Tyler or Boleyn
73 Adam's madam
74 Golfing Tom and namesakes
75 "Hey, pal!"
76 Shirt color for Tiger, often

DOWN

1 "Never mind!"
2 Put in one's two cents

3 Crucial Revolutionary War battle
4 Nav. rank
5 Leftover pizza from the office party, etc.
6 ___-Rooter
7 Pertaining to the eye
8 It might get stubbed
9 "___ So Shy"
10 Since
11 Actor Robert De ___
12 Pre-deal money
15 Vermont attraction
20 "Sprechen ___ Deutsch?"
22 That boat
25 Hoopsters' org.
27 Ending for orange
28 Watson et al.

30 Hit softly, as a ball onto the green
32 Teddy Roosevelt was one
33 Trigonometric measurement
34 Therefore
35 Pohl, Forsman, and Halldorson
36 Vicinity
38 Congressman, for short
41 Sale condition
43 Schoolyard game
46 Singer Yoko
48 ___-di-dah (pretentious)
51 ___ Antonio
53 Enjoy the 19th hole, maybe
55 Golf bag adjunct
57 Began the hole
58 Did some stitching
59 Floppy ___
60 Former Atlanta arena
61 Dalmatian feature
63 Also-___ (losers)
66 Wash. neighbor
67 Legal matter
69 After expenses

FOREST GRUMP

A golf legend's take on slices and hooks.

ACROSS

1 L.A. problem
5 Ladies' Tour player Hjorth
10 Sandler of "Happy Gilmore"
14 ___ Country Club (Hawaiian course)
15 ___ the run (grab something to go)
16 Actor Robert De ___
17 Start of a Lee Trevino quip
20 Pavarotti or Domingo
21 Trap stuff
22 He's got a sentence
23 Fail to roll, as a ball pitched onto the green
25 Jack Nicklaus and Tiger Woods
27 Quip, part 2
32 Year, to Sergio Garcia
33 Light ___ (almost weightless)
34 Is worth it
36 ___ 1 (the speed of sound)

40 Quip, part 3
41 Shore of tournaments
42 Resonating words
43 Stop, as tournament play
44 Gimme distance, maybe
45 It might be used as storage space
46 Inaccurate, like a putt
48 Quip, part 4
50 Loss of 1999
53 ___ roll (playing well)
54 Clubhouse drink
55 A cardinal point
59 It might flow through a course
63 End of the quip
67 Ireland, poetically
68 1976 Super Bowl MVP
69 1995 NL Rookie of the Year

70 Former Attorney General Janet
71 Announced as the winner, as of PGA Tour Player of the Year
72 Venturi and Green

DOWN

1 Enjoy Aspen
2 Castle surrounder
3 "This round's ___!"
4 Make progress (on), as a tournament leader
5 ___ system
6 Relaxer's sound
7 Hwys.
8 State where you'd find Cedar Rapids Golf Course
9 Nameless, for short

10 Pitch ___ putt (golf course variety)
11 '70s craze
12 Burning desire?
13 Crescent and half
18 Reply to a superior
19 Norse god of war
24 Make a very short putt
26 "The Iceman ___"
27 Tallying a scorecard, say
28 "He'll ___ six-iron for this shot ..." (commentator's line)
29 Say "fore!"
30 ___ Head, South Carolina (noted golf resort)
31 Lopez of the links
32 Burnt stuff
35 Shout after holing a great putt

37 Play's beginning
38 Fashionable
39 Scott of the PGA Tour
41 Discrepancy, casually
45 PGA Tour Rookie of the Year, e.g.
47 What putt distances are given in
49 Straighten out a club
50 ___ tiger
51 TV's "Kate & ___"
52 Long (for)
56 Part of PGA
57 ___ woman in half (perform a magic trick)
58 Mine car
60 Porker's grunt
61 Woodwind instrument
62 J-O binders
64 Prefix with classicism
65 Compass dir.
66 Goddess of the dawn

ANSWER, PAGE 83

AFTER JUNIOR

A foursome with family ties.

ACROSS

1 Jim of the Senior PGA Tour
5 ___ beam
10 Calendar abbr.
13 Ending for teen
14 Martini component
15 ___ fide
16 Only full-blooded Native American on the PGA Tour
18 Autobahn auto
19 Kind of twosome
20 "___ the Family"
21 World-___ (like some golfers or courses)
24 1997 PGA Championship winner
27 Tease
28 Seventh Greek letter
29 Actor Beatty
30 Joe or Jumbo
33 Practice ___
36 PGA Tour player whose father won the 1927 U.S. Open

39 ___ up (gets fit)
40 Skeleton pictures
43 ___-fi (literary category)
46 See 54-Across
47 What comes after the names of the four players featured herein
48 Multiple Buy.com Tour winner
52 Mardi and Karen of the LPGA
54 With 46-Across, Africa's top golfer
55 Lousy used car
57 Toiling
58 Strong tournament result ... or where each of the theme entries stands in family lineage
63 Actress Moreno of "West Side Story"

64 Pertaining to birth
65 Aoki of the Senior PGA Tour
66 Point opposite NNW
67 "If you don't, ___ will!"
68 Handy golf advice

DOWN

1 Forsman of the PGA Tour
2 Tiger's lack
3 Make after expenses
4 Hole headaches
5 Wolf, in Guatemala
6 Has ___ over (is beating)
7 Eleven letters after 28-Across
8 Dahllof of the Ladies' Tour

9 San Luis ___ Downs (San Diego golf resort)
10 Eldridge Cleaver book "___ Ice"
11 Salad veggie
12 Hurt
15 Titleist product
17 "48 ___"
20 Strong ___ (like John Daly)
21 ___-Magnon
22 Taylor or Claiborne
23 Blind as ___
25 Changes course, as a ball in flight
26 Thing
31 Sends to the canvas, slangily
32 Arriver's announcement
33 Fleetwood Mac hit
34 Charlotte of "The Facts of Life"

35 Big ___ (town south of Pebble Beach)
37 Bad, to Sergio Garcia
38 Play stopper
41 Yang's counterpart
42 Sib for bro
43 Obtains wool
44 Strange on the links
45 Turn on, as a barbecue
49 ___ wedge (pitch)
50 The best of the best
51 Showed over
52 Cut (off)
53 Like some candles
56 1551, to ancient Romans
58 Explosive letters
59 Derisive cry
60 "___ see it ..."
61 Tiger's says Nike
62 Goddess identified with Aurora

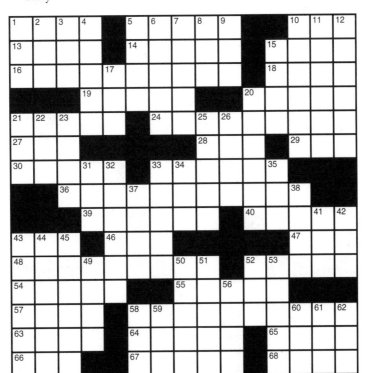

ANSWER, PAGE 85

OPEN SPACES

America is full of them.

ACROSS

1 Scary Stephen King dog
5 Volkswagen's Golf, and others
9 Native American pole
14 ___ arms (irate)
15 End in ___ (require a playoff)
16 Make ___ of (pay attention to)
17 Site of Lee Janzen's first U.S. Open win in 1993
19 Las Vegas lights
20 City where you'll find the Peachtree Golf Club
21 Site of 45-year-old Hale Irwin's remarkable win at the 1990 U.S. Open
23 Putts ___ hole (PGA stat)
24 Mildred Zaharias, familiarly
25 Like John Daly's drives
28 Cast one's ballot
30 1998 PGA Tour Player of the Year
35 "There was an old woman who lived in ___"
37 Besides
39 Story line

40 Treacherous course where Corey Pavin's even-par 280 was enough to win the 1995 U.S. Open
43 ___ avail (uselessly)
44 Astronomy wonder
45 School: French
46 Kept for later
48 Classic Jane Austen work
50 British Open break
51 ___ Hole (17th at St. Andrews)
53 Microbrew, maybe
55 Pennsylvania course that's hosted many U.S. Opens
59 Duplicate functions

63 Fibber's admission
64 Ohio course that's hosted four U.S. Opens, most recently in 1979
66 Starbucks order
67 Extremely dangerous, as a hole
68 Affliction suffix
69 Three-time U.S. Open runner-up
70 They may be electric
71 ___ Lake Golf Club (site of the Tour Championship)

DOWN

1 Country that's home to the El Veradero Golf Club

2 ___ the crack of dawn (rising for an early tee time, maybe)
3 McGill of the LPGA Tour
4 Like some beer
5 Despot from 1-Down
6 Big name in razors
7 Brazilian destination
8 Alabama city
9 Bicycle built for two
10 "The ___ Love"
11 "Who Framed Roger Rabbit" character
12 Sicilian peak
13 Interlock
18 Inconsistent, as putting
22 Online reading experience

24 Like Jack Nicklaus, to fans
25 Doesn't eat
26 Have ___ at (be in the running for)
27 Beast with a horn on its snout
29 Tex-Mex snack
31 Long tale
32 Set aside
33 Esther of "Good Times"
34 Sailing the waves
36 ___ about (approximately)
38 The Pigeon Drop, e.g.
41 Finish with
42 Faith ___
47 Disappeared slowly, as a lead
49 Self-proclaimed experts
52 One at ___
54 Mr. Els
55 Sesame and peanut
56 Bratton of the PGA Tour
57 U.S. Open winner of 1992
58 Physical start
59 Racecourse shape
60 "___ Smile Be Your Umbrella"
61 Garage sale words
62 "Hey, you!"
65 Wedding announcement word

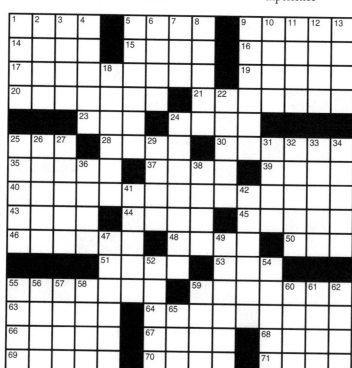

ANSWER, PAGE 87

THE BRITISH OPEN

Focusing on the Brits, dear fellow.

ACROSS

1 Be cautious on the links
6 Requiring a playoff round
10 Corn or oats
14 Tinker to ___ to Chance (famed baseball double play)
15 Razors name
16 Improbable 1964 British Open champ
17 Winner of the first British Open
19 "Would you like ___ with that?" (drugstore question)
20 Society's problems
21 Zero, in soccer
22 Gladiator's milieu
23 ___ Paulo, Brazil
24 His British Open triumph of 1969 was the first by a Briton in 18 years
27 It will give you a soft lie
28 Busy as ___
29 "I'm such an ___!" (golf course self-reproach)
32 Soap ingredient
33 ___-Am

36 He won the 2nd, 3rd, 5th, and 8th British Opens; his son won the next four after that
41 Snake common in Egypt
42 Alley-___
43 "The Legend of Bagger ___" (2000 golf movie starring Matt Damon and Will Smith)
44 Gogel of the Tour
46 Part of a process
48 His 1934 British Open win put a halt to American domination of the event
52 Golden State sch.
55 Make ___ for oneself
56 Exist

57 Regarding
58 Nincompoop
59 Member of "The Triumvirate" who won five British Opens between 1901 and 1910
62 "How did ___ that happen?"
63 Brain output
64 Tiger's goal on a par five
65 ___ chips (trendy snack food)
66 Enjoy the sun
67 Fabric you might see at St. Andrews

DOWN

1 Tour player J.L.
2 1950s baseball star Bobby
3 Mello ___ (soft drink brand)
4 Net addresses

5 Next-to-last Greek letter
6 Easy putts
7 Costantino Rocca's homeland
8 Commit a blunder
9 S. ___ (Nebr. neighbor)
10 Big name in Irish golf
11 James Dean's image
12 Certain Arab
13 Heathen
18 "Dukes of Hazzard" spinoff
22 Links rarity
24 Dorothy's dog
25 Haas and Don Blake of the Tour
26 Lincoln and Vigoda
27 Many an LPGA Tour player
29 "Give ___ try!"

30 Two for Sergio
31 Mischief maker
32 Cup's edge
33 ___ placement
34 Fox sitcom of the 1990s
35 It's mined
37 "Weekend Warriors" group
38 ___-Rooter
39 With nothing but pars
40 Take a snooze
44 Movie role for Peter Lorre
45 Yes, at sea
46 Winning ___
47 Shoe residents
48 "I've ___ up to here ..."
49 ___ Gay (plane that dropped the atomic bomb)
50 2000 election hopeful
51 Brings under control, as the yips
52 Grammar concern
53 Ending for turn
54 Like wartime messages
57 Get ___ deal
59 Kind of triangular sail
60 Letters on many tubes of toothpaste
61 People do it a lot on putts in "Caddyshack"

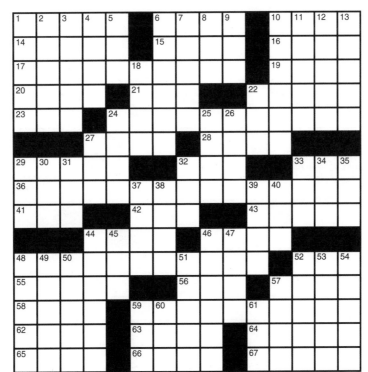

ANSWER, PAGE 89

73

G'DAY, AMERICA!

And to this trio of stars.

ACROSS

1 City that draws crowds
6 North Carolina college
10 Course vehicle
14 Book for travelers
15 TV's "Warrior Princess"
16 High male voice
17 With 41- and 65-Across, the stars of this puzzle
20 It might be broken on a drive
21 Listening device?
22 Tit for ___
23 Star #1
27 Star #2
31 Part of PGA
32 Takes to court
34 Cousin of the clarinet
35 Half a famous first name in golf
38 It may make your shot tougher
40 ___ others play through

41 See 17-Across
44 Suffix with Manhattan
46 Plantation in "Gone With the Wind"
47 ___ kwon do
48 A golfer may remove it from the green before putting
50 Hit perfectly, as a drive
52 Gets along in years
56 Actress ___ Jessica Parker
58 Remains faithful
61 Sought office
63 ___ double take
64 "I'd like to buy ___" ("Wheel of Fortune" statement)
65 See 17-Across
71 Not for

72 Fully mature female horse
73 Investigate, as a phone call
74 Arizona Indian tribe
75 They might clash
76 Prepared to putt

DOWN

1 Kathy of country music
2 Merman and Barrymore
3 One-irons of old
4 Tiger, for example
5 Pale
6 Puts forth, as effort
7 Mr. Trevino
8 ___ roll (doing well)
9 Of the sea: Abbr.
10 Caribbean dictator

11 "The Greatest" boxer
12 Hwy.
13 Lean-___ (housing structures)
18 You can wipe your ball off with it
19 Get droopy
24 Gimme measurement
25 Be more patient than
26 He fiddled while Rome burned
28 With the skills
29 John or Jane
30 Up to this point
33 Used the mail
36 Winning a lot
37 John, in Russia
39 Seventh letter, in Athens
41 Big name in Canadian golf

42 Periods in the past
43 It can affect a golfer's performance
44 "___ going to go long" (golf announcer's line)
45 Delta competitor
49 Woods rival
51 Part of LPGA
53 Star #3
54 ___ Kennedy Shriver
55 Did some oozing
57 "Yeah, right!"
59 "___-hoo!"
60 He may bring you golf clubs late in the year
62 Scorecard info
65 Fork over the dough
66 Animal that doesn't sound old?
67 You'll need your PIN to use it
68 "Golf Digest," for example
69 ___-Am
70 ___ Lanka

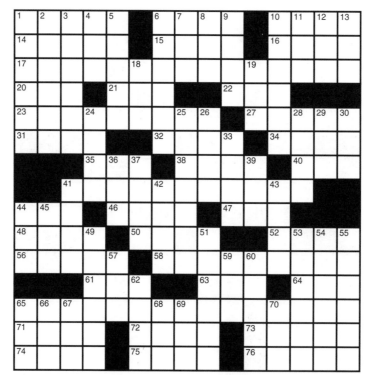

ANSWER, PAGE 91

A MAJOR PLAYER

All about David Toms.

ACROSS

1 Be a copycat
4 Take out of the freezer
8 Fall in the rankings
12 What fans shouldn't be while a player is putting
14 An executive course has nine
16 Simon & Garfunkel's "___ Rock"
17 City where David Toms lives
19 Marvel comic book characters
20 Where Toms was an All-American
22 Black or Red
23 Rain may cause it
24 Vicente Fernandez's country: Abbr.
27 You may get some while playing golf
29 Kind of clause: Abbr.
30 Tiger Woods and David Duval

33 Lack of many phones
35 Golfer McKelvey
37 Mecca resident
39 Toms's first PGA Tour victory, in 1997
43 ___ par
44 Water, in Quebec
45 Mild swear heard on the course
46 Sponsors get to run them
47 Female bleater
50 A-E connection
52 Main and Elm: Abbr.
53 Clearwater of the Tour
55 Beats in the ring, for short
57 One of two tournaments won by Toms in 1999
63 "Rules of Golf" org.

64 1992 tournament where Toms started with a record-tying 63
66 Early-morning golf course visitor
67 Punches hard
68 Hay amount
69 Tests on which 1600 is perfect
70 Places to eat well and exercise
71 Direction away from NNE

DOWN

1 Geiberger and others
2 Dan on the Tour
3 Money for Langer or Garcia
4 Synonym books
5 Southwestern Indian tribe
6 Take ___ off (relax)

7 Klemperer of "Hogan's Heroes"
8 Very rare score for 18 holes
9 Dalai ___
10 "Haven't ___ you somewhere before?"
11 Window part
13 God, to the ancient Romans
15 Like hard bread
18 Gets competitive
21 Chips go-with
24 Water, in Milan
25 18 holes
26 Alumni
28 Word that changes the entire meaning of a sentence
30 Calliope, Terpsichore, et al.
31 Order from above
32 Price and Faldo

34 President after HST
36 Tournament freebie
38 ___ Wednesday
40 Flowing course hazard
41 It's hailed in cities
42 Unfortunate
48 Candle parts
49 Merman and Barrymore
51 Suffix with evil
53 Some Chryslers
54 Overplay, as a role
56 Person too good for others
57 Future flowers
58 "He's going to ___ three-iron here ..." (golf announcer's line)
59 "Now ___ it!"
60 Org. for Pak
61 High school nos.
62 Slithery fish
65 Compaq Classic of ___ Orleans (Toms Tour victory of 2001)

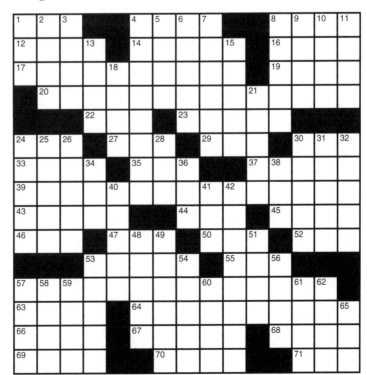

FABULOUS '50S

The mid-century in golf.

ACROSS

1 Fail to sink the putt
5 Resort city of western England
9 '52 U.S. Open winner Julius
14 Mr. Mickelson
18 Japanese senior Aoki
19 Too assertive
20 Make adjustments
21 Hamlet or Othello
22 PGA leading money winner of '53
24 U.S. Women's Open champ of '51, '53, and '57
26 Shed type
27 Two-time U.S. Open winner Els
29 Spy novelist Deighton
30 Playoff causers
32 Nicholas or Ivan
35 Surround completely
39 Continue, as a tradition
42 Artist
45 '92 Literature Nobelist Walcott
46 Fairway liners, often
47 Classic time?
49 Hemmed and ___ (stalled for time)
51 No, to Robert Burns
52 Loathe
53 Masters site
55 Masters winner of '57
58 Scott Turow book about Harvard Law School
59 Canadian Indian tribe
60 "King Kong" star Fay
62 Movie holders
63 Polite address
64 Riches' counterparts
65 53, to Caesar
66 With ___ breath (expectantly)
67 Have a hero
68 Fuss
69 Where to say you do
70 Seventh Greek letter
71 Actress Dawber of "Mork & Mindy"
74 Seedy place to live
76 Pencil and paper game
77 In a ___ (huffy)
78 Anagram and past tense of 67-Across
79 Indian pole
80 "___ sow, so shall ..."
81 Santa syllables
82 Dog bane
83 Masters winner of '52 and '54
85 "You gotta be kidding!"
87 Middle Eastern nation
88 Stomach muscles
89 Power for Fulton
91 Two-time British Open winner Norman
92 "Give it ___!"
93 Swim meet sites
96 Hodgepodge
98 Current unit
100 Beethoven work, sometimes
102 Clinton cabinet member
103 Piece of cake
104 Dem.'s rival
105 Big name in Swedish cinema
108 Late-night giant
113 British Open winner of '59
119 British Open winner of '50, '52, and '57
121 Ugandan strongman
122 Swahili for "freedom"
123 Chicago squad
124 Ripped
125 Big cat that sounds like a golf course
126 Bad city for witches
127 Editor's mark
128 Celebrity

DOWN

1 Factory
2 Phrase of understanding
3 ___ woman in half (perform some magic)
4 Planted
5 Jackson and Diddley
6 Fireplace remnants
7 32-Across, another way
8 Church song
9 U.S. Women's Open champ of '50 and '54
10 Praising poem
11 Tell the fuzz
12 Photo-___ (politicians' publicity sessions)
13 Flair
14 Frolic
15 Reporter's question
16 Under the weather
17 Bandleader Brown
19 Oven setting
23 Preminger and von Bismarck
25 Tear asunder
28 Clinch, as a victory
31 U.S. Open winner of '54
33 ___ standstill (stuck)
34 Loud and misbehaving
36 Masters winner of '58
37 Roebuck partner
38 ___ out a living
39 Muse of astronomy
40 British Open winner of '54, '55, '56, and '58
41 Shoe part
42 Hint for Holmes
43 "Treasure Island" author's initials
44 Classic automobile letters
46 Yonder items
48 Gets better, as wine
50 Time span
53 Colleges, pretentiously
54 Giggle
56 Insinuate
57 Lawyer's charge
61 Eagle's place
64 Poe creature
65 PGA leading money winner of '51
66 U.S. Open winner of '50, '51, and '53
69 Classifieds
72 General's "relax!"
73 Tried to say
75 Extra sporting periods: Abbr.
77 Not all
79 No-no
80 "Doe, ___ ..."
81 Loser to the tortoise
82 Cry on a bad slice
83 Drains of energy
84 Modern cash source
86 Omelet component
90 Nineteenth hole beverage
92 Shock and disappoint
94 Voice box
95 Plan part
97 Neither/___
99 Noted NYC store
101 Greatest grade
103 Nice fur
106 Wanes
107 Trumpet
109 Goes to the dogs
110 Troon resident
111 Gumbo veggie
112 ___-do-well
113 Guy's pal
114 Women's star Alcott
115 ___ Tin Tin
116 "Just as I suspected!"
117 "The King and I" name
118 Before, poetically
120 Diner order

GETTING OFFICIAL

No nicknames allowed.

ACROSS

1 Person in charge
5 Go a few rounds
9 Go after the ball
14 "___ my wit's end!"
15 Grow weary
16 Place for some furniture
17 Clinton official Federico
18 Rent-___
19 Most Middle Easterners
20 Tiger, officially
23 Article for Langer
24 Manhattan sch.
25 Wish you hadn't
26 Mr. Crenshaw
29 Workers at an event
31 It may be a gimme
33 Model MacPherson
34 Carry, like a caddy does a golf bag
36 Bk. of the Bible
37 Throw in the towel
38 Chi Chi, officially
42 Like par-5s
43 "The Simpsons" character
44 More than bi-
45 Garage sale words
46 On ___ (how some articles are written)
48 Kitchen wear
52 Up to now
53 Stock event, for short
54 Mel of slugging
56 Lennon's lady
57 Fuzzy, officially

60 Martinez on the mound
63 City of Oklahoma
64 "There oughta be ___!"
65 Space visitor
66 Have to have
67 Monster of the Southwest
68 They can affect your ball
69 Actress Harper
70 Just

DOWN

1 Humans, for instance
2 Brunch food
3 Actress Bernhardt
4 Constellation member
5 Actor Keach
6 Concede the hole
7 Three in ___
8 Sports journalist, say
9 Card design
10 Korean and Vietnam
11 "Give ___ rest!"
12 Pen tip
13 Signals to proceed
21 Jokingly
22 Drive longer than
26 Color of some tees
27 English queen: Abbr.
28 Driving range border
30 Hole markers
32 Like some criticism
33 Deck out
35 "If you can't ___ simple concept ..."
38 "No way, ___!"
39 Apartment, to real estate agents

40 The other guy
41 Work with parmesan
42 ___ up
47 Teapot covers
49 Find the hole
50 Possible score after two holes in a head-to-head match
51 Country noted for its "Midnight Golf"
53 Bag choices
55 Bridges and Eldredge
57 Mr. Couples
58 It bends slightly on your swing
59 Lake, in Mexico
60 Dog's offering
61 ___ Lilly
62 Noise

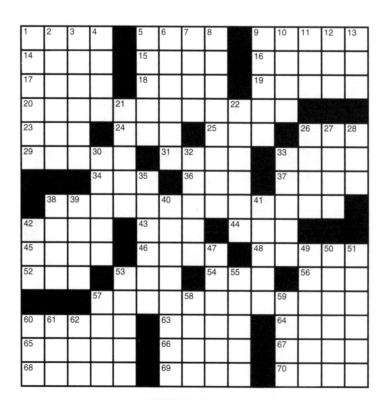

6 THE ROARING '20S

```
L A C E ■ S A L T ■ ■ P A W S ■ ■
O P E N ■ T R E E ■ ■ S N A P S ■
L E O D I E G E L ■ ■ I G L O O ■
■ ■ ■ S T R O K E S ■ ■ E T O N ■
S T S ■ A N N ■ ■ A L L E N S ■ ■
T O T A L S ■ S E N I O R ■ ■ ■ ■
A R E M Y ■ S P A D E ■ ■ H O P ■
I M E T ■ S T O R Y ■ ■ D A N A ■
D E L ■ F E A R S ■ ■ B O G E Y ■
■ S E R E N E ■ ■ H O L E I N ■ ■
L E H M A N ■ ■ M O O ■ N N E ■ ■
A R A B ■ O A K M O N T ■ ■ ■ ■ ■
R A F E R ■ W A L K E R C U P ■ ■
A S T R O ■ E R I E ■ ■ A U T O ■
■ E S S O ■ S L I D ■ ■ P E E P ■
```

15 MM NUMBERS, PART 2

```
R E N T S ■ H E M ■ ■ A P P A L ■
A D A P T ■ E M U ■ ■ M I A M I ■
N A N C Y R A M S B O T T O M ■ ■
S M U ■ O R A T O R ■ ■ E K E ■ ■
■ ■ A L O T ■ ■ L A P ■ ■ ■ ■ ■
D O R O T H Y D E L A S I N ■ ■ ■
M O P E S ■ A I R ■ ■ W E R E ■ ■
A N T ■ S H E L D O N ■ V W S ■ ■
A T I T ■ E L I ■ ■ O N E I S ■ ■
M I C H E L L E M C G A N N ■ ■ ■
■ E V E ■ ■ O U S T ■ ■ ■ ■ ■ ■
T O A ■ O N E F O R ■ ■ I N A ■ ■
A N N I K A S O R E N S T A M ■ ■
L E A V E ■ P R E ■ ■ B I T T E ■
K I T E S ■ N E D ■ ■ C R O O N ■
```

24 FROM THE CLUBHOUSE ...

```
T A F T ■ O N C E A ■ ■ J A W ■
A C R O ■ R O L L S ■ ■ T O D O ■
G E O R G E B U S H ■ ■ O H I O ■
■ ■ E A G L E ■ ■ E A R N E D ■ ■
E B B ■ M O E ■ ■ A S K U S ■ ■
D R I V E N ■ M O N R O E ■ ■ ■
D A L E S ■ T U L I P ■ ■ N F L ■
I S L E ■ F E D E X ■ ■ O N E I ■
E S C ■ M E L D S ■ ■ S I E V E ■
■ L O U D L Y ■ ■ G O L D E N ■ ■
S K I N S ■ C A L ■ ■ Y R S ■ ■
T O N I T E ■ O L L I E ■ ■ ■ ■
O R T O ■ G E R A L D F O R D ■
P E O N ■ G R I P E ■ ■ G R A Y ■
S A N ■ S A S S Y ■ ■ H O P E ■
```

33 TRAGIC TRIVIA

```
M A D A M ■ T A T E ■ ■ B A R R ■
A S O R E ■ A L I E ■ ■ O H I O ■
W H A T G O L F E R ■ ■ B O O S ■
S Y S ■ A H E A D ■ ■ E M P T Y ■
■ ■ A T O N ■ ■ A B A ■ ■ ■ ■ ■
H A S L O S T A P L A Y O F F ■ ■
A K E E N ■ ■ D A L Y ■ R A E ■ ■
I R E S ■ P A I R S ■ ■ F O R E ■
T O S ■ C U T E ■ ■ T U N E D ■ ■
I N A L L F O U R M A J O R S ■ ■
■ A U F ■ A O K I ■ ■ ■ ■ ■ ■ ■
P L A N B ■ C A N O E ■ ■ I C E ■
L O N G ■ G R E G N O R M A N ■ ■
A N N E ■ M E R E ■ ■ F O U N D ■
Y E A R ■ T W O S ■ ■ F I S T S ■
```

7 THE 59ERS

```
ROYAL  BECK    ABS
IRENE  ERIE  FLEE
NOTAHBEGAY  AGRA
    MARS  SPLEEN
JED  ANS    EDITS
AROUND  HOBNOB
NOUNS  TEXAS  ENG
EDGE  HOLED  CREE
TED  LINEN  FUGUE
  USOPEN  LITERS
LINKS    FEE  ROE
AWAITS  ORAL
TAKE  DAVIDDUVAL
USER  ARES  EVITA
SAY    KIRK  DANES
```

16 72ND IN '75

```
EST    SCAR  JONES
LOCH  LANE  EVENT
INCA  ALDA  READY
JOHNNYMILLER
ARESO    MOM  HUE
HAN  WHOA  BYPASS
  VIENNA  OLES
  TOMWEISKOPF
TAUT  SNEEZE
SPREAD  ETNA  SIL
PEN  ZOO  RANGE
  JACKNICKLAUS
CAROL  RICH  ERAS
ARISE  ALOE  GENE
MEDEA  SENT  DAN
```

25 WHERE TO THIS YEAR ...

```
WAS  SEEIT  PETER
ICI  NAGLE  ARUDE
STGEORGES  LARGE
HOME  LYTHAM  NED
  FALDO    SERB
  OFF  SPRYEST
JAPAN  ONCE  DRAW
ECRU  TROON  ERIA
FLED  EDIT  DRYLY
FUSIONS  SCI
  TOTS    HEDGE
SOW  HEARME  ALLI
PRICE  MUIRFIELD
OCCUR  OLLIE  NIL
TAKES  SELES  SSE
```

34 YOU SAID A MOUTHFUL!

```
SALES  BRAGS  TIP
CRAVE  RENEW  WOO
AMMACCAPANE  OWN
LOA  TAN  TED  PAY
ERRS  PCS    EAU
  HETHERINGTON
  IMON  AIR  ETNA
STU  GRASPED  EMP
ISLA  ELI    RIDE
CALCAVECCHIA
  IER    KIM  NAST
BIG  ALI  DOS  CHE
ADA  BALLESTEROS
BON  IDLER  AGENT
ELS  ASSES  ROSES
```

42 WHAT ABOUT BOB?

```
J A N E   S H I N S   A B C S
A L O G   T O T A L   I R O N
B I N G C R O S B Y   N I L E
    S H A K Y   L I T T L E
A R M   E Y E   G Y M   I S R
W A Y N E   R B I   G A S
A N G O R A   R R S   C H I
Y A R D   S A U L T   T O R I
  T E E   S B C   U S O P E N
  E S T   L E D   A R E N T
I O N   A C E   E R R   N E O
D U F F E R   A S I A N
O N E A   E I S E N H O W E R
I C E S   S T A R K   P A T E
T E S T   T E N T S   E D A M
```

51 HEAVY METAL

```
M I A M I   T A G   I T A L
I N T E L   A R I A   O H N O
S T E E L S H A F T   U R N S
S E A T   H O T T E A   E S T
A R M   J O E   S E E
    P O P   B A C K N I N E
B O G E Y   F A C E   T R A P
A P O P   T O K E N   R O M E
K E L P   A R E S   R E N E E
U N D E R P A R   H O E
  M R S   D O N   I S T
A B E   T I N C U P   I N T O
B I D E   S I L V E R S C O T
E T A L   O N E A   I T A K E
E E L S   A O L   M O S E S
```

60 IT'S IN THE BAG!

```
K E M P E R   B U S   D A B
A R O U S E   W A S H   A W E
L I S T E N   E D G E   V E T
  E S T   E D D   A R M I E S
    E M E R G E   R I S K Y
S P I R E   S E N T I N
M A N A G E   O N A   N A S H
U S S R   R A F E R   I L I E
G O T O   A R C   S L E A Z E
    U P S T H E   E D S E L
A R E N A   S E N I O R
S A N D R A   E D S   I N K
I N D   R U T S   L E V I E S
A G O   E D I E   A V E N E L
N E W   D I N   M E R E L Y
```

69 THE TERRAIN GAME

```
B O B   A F R O   T H A N A
A P U   D R O P   G O E S I N
G I N   M I T T   R E S O R T
I N K S   N O I S E   F O E
T E E I N G   C H E A T
  R E B E L   E N D O R S E
D A H   A B A R   M E M O I R
A R I A   E Y E T O   S U N G
N E L S O N   P A U L   G E O
S A L I N E S   G N A S H
  S O F A S   T H I R D S
D O S   I N T R A   T I R E
I M P O R T   R A I N   D O W
S N O R E S   A N N E   E V E
K I T E S   P S S T   R E D
```

8 WORKING THE SWING SHIFT

M	A	J	O	R		A	D	L	I	B		P	A	R
A	S	I	D	E		B	A	Y	O	U		I	S	O
T	I	M	E	D		E	V	E	N	T		N	E	A
T	A	M	S		D	A	I	S		C	L	E	A	R
E	N	C		F	O	R	D		C	H	E	S	T	S
	L	U	L	U		L	E	C	H	E				
T	R	E	M	O	R		E	L	L	A		R	I	P
S	O	A	P	Y		H	A	S		R	E	I	N	S
P	E	N		D	E	A	D		S	M	A	C	K	S
	T	H	U	M	B		W	O	R	K				
S	E	N	I	O	R		E	V	A	N		S	A	O
T	R	U	E	R		S	T	E	M		O	M	I	T
I	N	D		G	R	A	T	E		A	F	I	S	H
L	I	E		E	A	G	E	R		T	I	T	L	E
L	E	S		N	E	A	R	S		E	T	H	E	R

17 A TRADITIONAL EDUCATION

A	F	A	R		W	H	I	S	T		G	A	M	E
P	O	L	E		C	A	N	O	E		O	P	A	L
S	C	O	T	T	S	D	A	L	E		L	A	D	S
E	I	E	I	O		A	N	D	I		F	R	E	E
			E	L	S		N	O	S					
	D	E	F	E	N	D	I	N	G	C	H	A	M	P
M	R	S		T	O	R	T	E		T	O	T	A	L
R	O	T	C		B	E	T	H	E		P	A	S	A
E	V	E	R	T		A	O	R	T	A		R	O	Y
D	E	S	E	R	T	M	O	U	N	T	A	I	N	
	N	I	A			A	O	L						
A	M	O	S		R	Y	A	N		O	P	E	R	A
W	A	S	H		G	A	R	Y	P	L	A	Y	E	R
E	L	L	A		E	L	I	S	E		C	E	N	T
S	L	O	W		T	E	P	E	E		A	D	D	S

26 MADE IN THE SHADE

C	A	N	O	N		T	U	T	O	R		S	O	N
A	D	O	R	E		A	R	E	N	A		U	N	O
R	O	N	N	I	E	B	L	A	C	K		T	I	T
	A	G	E	S		S	U	E		T	O	M		
E	A	R	T	H	S		S	E	E		Z	O	N	E
S	H	O	E		F	T	S		B	E	N	S		
P	A	N		P	A	I	R		A	I	R			
	B	I	L	L	Y	R	A	Y	B	R	O	W	N	
	P	U	N		N	E	E	D		H	I	T		
	L	O	G	S		P	G	A		K	A	N	E	
M	A	M	A		T	E	E		A	B	A	T	E	D
O	W	E		C	O	B		O	P	E	R			
I	R	A		H	U	B	E	R	T	G	R	E	E	N
S	I	R		I	S	L	A	M		A	I	S	L	E
T	E	A		P	E	E	T	E		Y	E	S	I	T

35 THIS AND THAT

M	A	K	E	S		B	A	L	L	S		T	R	I
A	S	A	V	E		O	N	E	A	L		R	O	D
T	H	R	E	E	A	N	D	T	W	O		U	S	E
T	O	M		S	A	Y	S		P	R	E	S	S	
S	T	A	I	R	S			G	E	E				
	G	E	T	U	P	A	N	D	D	O	W	N		
T	A	H	O	E		T	A	D	A		S	H	O	E
R	N	A		F	A	U	C	E	T	S		M	R	S
A	T	R	A		T	R	E	E		E	A	S	E	S
P	I	T	C	H	A	N	D	P	U	T	T			
	R	O	N			S	A	L	A	M	I			
H	A	G	E	N		F	U	J	I		D	I	D	
A	L	L		C	H	I	P	A	N	D	R	O	L	L
A	T	E		H	O	N	O	R		E	A	G	L	E
S	O	N		O	P	E	N	S		E	S	S	E	S

43 STARTING ... SEVENTEENTH

E	V	A	N	S		M	E	D	I	A		F	O	G
S	O	L	I	D		A	R	E	N	T		O	H	O
Q	U	A	L	I	F	Y	I	N	G	R	O	U	N	D
S	S	W			O	A	K			E	U	R	O	S
		B	A	R			T	H	A	T				
Q	U	A	R	T	E	R	S	H	O	T		M	A	S
U	N	T	I	E		A	C	E	S		B	A	C	H
A	D	O	G		S	N	O	R	E		E	Z	R	A
K	E	N	S		O	K	R	A		O	R	D	E	R
E	R	E		Q	U	I	E	T	P	L	E	A	S	E
		B	U	R	N			R	E	T				
A	T	S	E	A		F	R	O			N	E	T	
Q	U	A	D	R	U	P	L	E	B	O	G	E	Y	S
U	R	N		T	R	E	E	S		L	A	U	R	A
A	N	D		S	L	E	E	T		D	I	N	E	R

52 THAT'S A LIE!

S	A	F	E	T	Y		H	O	C	H		O	N	S
I	N	A	R	E	D		O	G	R	E		R	O	T
D	A	V	I	E	S		P	L	A	Y	A	B	L	E
	O	N	O		F	E	E	T		B	I	T	E	
S	I	R		F	A	R		D	E	B	A	T	E	D
A	H	A		F	R	E	T		R	E	T			
N	E	B			I	S	I	T		R	E	P	E	L
G	A	L		H	A	N	G	I	N	G		R	A	Y
A	R	E	S	O		O	H	N	O		E	R	R	
		A	P	B		T	I	P	S		F	E	E	
B	E	A	T	S	U	P		E	E	K		E	D	S
O	M	N	I		R	O	A	R		A	P	R		
D	O	W	N	H	I	L	L		S	T	A	R	E	D
E	R	A		B	E	E	P		H	E	L	E	N	A
S	Y	R		O	D	D	S		E	R	O	D	E	D

61 SOUNDS LIKE A GOLFER

A	P	S	O		T	E	C	H		S	B	C
U	S	E	S	A		A	T	R	A	S		A	L	A
K	I	T	C	H	E	N	C	I	N	K		H	U	G
		A	O	L		E	D	Y		I	R	E
	W	O	R	L	D	W	I	D	E	W	E	B	B
S	E	Z		D	E	E	R		R	A	M
P	L	A	Y		R	I	O	T		R	O	S	S	I
A	S	K	E	D		R	N	A		D	R	O	P	S
R	H	I	N	O		D	I	R	E		Y	U	A	N
		T	O	M		N	O	T	S		S	N	O
	L	E	A	D	I	N	G	T	H	E	P	A	K
M	E	A		A	D	O		N	E	A
E	G	G		D	A	L	Y	D	O	U	B	L	E	S
G	A	L		S	I	T	E	S		S	L	I	C	E
A	L	E		R	E	S	T		O	D	O	R

70 FOREST GRUMP

S	M	O	G		M	A	R	I	A		A	D	A	M
K	O	N	A		E	A	T	O	N		N	I	R	O
I	A	M	I	N	T	H	E	W	O	O	D	S	S	O
	T	E	N	O	R		S	A	N	D		C	O	N
		S	I	T				I	C	O	N	S
M	U	C	H	I	C	A	N		A	N	O
A	S	A	I	R		P	A	Y	S		M	A	C	H
T	E	L	L		D	I	N	A	H		E	C	H	O
H	A	L	T		I	N	C	H		A	T	T	I	C
		O	F	F		Y	O	U	W	H	I	C	H
P	A	Y	N	E			O	N	A
A	L	E		E	A	S	T		B	R	O	O	K
P	L	A	N	T	S	A	R	E	E	D	I	B	L	E
E	I	R	E		S	W	A	N	N		N	O	M	O
R	E	N	O		N	A	M	E	D		K	E	N	S

9 HAVING A BALL

```
R U T H   B L A D E     G E R
I S E E   L O C A L   L U R E
B A L A T A B A L L   A T R A
      V I S O R   S A U T E D
A F F E C T       B R A D S
L I O N S   M I S H A P
P L U S   T H A T T O   E S C
H E R   L E A T H E R   R E A
A S H   A S L E E P   S C A N
  U N I T E D     E T H N O
A M N O T       A T E A S E
R E D E Y E   B I T T E
E A R L   F E A T H E R I E S
O D E S   G A R B O   E S P N
N E D   H U E Y S   R A I L
```

18 FIRST THINGS FIRST

```
D A N A   A F E W   O F A
O V E R   D A D A   W A R N
T O M M O R R I S S E N I O R
O N O   B E R T H A     S T U
    P E A       B A N T A M
L E F T Y M A J O R C H A M P
A R E A S   R E H E E L
W A Y   S A W A S     E S E
    R A P I E R   S H E L L
S E V E B A L L E S T E R O S
E V A D E R     P E R
L E I   T A M P E R   S P A
A N N I K A S O R E N S T A M
  T E R I   A R O D   E A S Y
  R A M   N E S S   A R T S
```

27 NIZHONI!

```
A D V I L   F O R K   F I B
S U I T E   S U S I E   I M A
F E D E X S T J U D E   F A T
A T E M   L E I   P I T C H
R O O   L O W   N E E D Y
    P O W   T O R R A N C E
L E W I S   D A V E   I I I
E V A N S   U P A   C O N A N
M E L   A V E S   O R E O S
A R K A N S A S   R I G
  E M A I L   F A N   P A R
P A R T V   R A G   T I M E
A R C   A L B U Q U E R Q U E
S M U   J E A N S   S E U S S
T S P   O D D S   P E E T E
```

36 EASY RYDER

```
J E F F   I N C H   A T B A T
A S I A   N O R A   C H E E R
W O R C E S T E R   S A N G A
    T R E A D E R   I C E D
C I A   A C H   S E I   R A E
A T B E S T     A T T E N D
S T E V E   S I M P S O N
H O M E   G E N U S   T S P S
  I R E L A N D   M E H O W
B A T T L E     F E M A L E
A N C   S A P   S E T   W E D
H I H O   M A S T E R S
A M E S S   T H E B E L F R Y
M A L L S   H E A L   I D E A
A L L O W   S A M E   M A C K
```

44 OUT OF AFRICA

```
E F L A T · B L O W · P A U L
A R O M A · R A N A · U S G A
G A R Y P L A Y E R · B A H S
L I D S · O N S · N I L · · ·
E L S · I N C · · D I S C S ·
· · H U G H B A I O C C H I ·
A L L E M · A W O L · H U T ·
L A I R · R I S E N · E M M A
E Y E · B E N S · F R O S T ·
R E T I E F G O O S E N · · ·
T R O O N · · U T Z · M I L ·
· · · W T A · A T A · T U N E
S A G A · B O B B Y L O C K E
U P O N · A L L I · O T H E R
N E T S · T E E D · W O O D S
```

53 AUTHOR, AUTHOR!

```
K O N A · G R A S S · · P I P
E W E S · R A D I O · A G R A
L E E T R E V I N O · T W O S
· · · R O G E R · T A L O N S
· A T I T · D E E · D A D S ·
A B O D E S · · T H O S E · ·
S A M E · W A S H E R · H U M
I B M · B O B H O P E · O N E
M A Y · E R N E S T · S U I T
· A G R E E · · A S K S T O
T R O T · R E F · T I E S ·
M I M O S A · T I R E D · ·
A T O N · J O H N U P D I K E
P L U S · A R E A S · E V I L
S E R · R O L L S · D E M S
```

62 IN MEMORIAM

```
S H O O T · R I L E Y · S H S
C A I R O · A C U R E · T I N
A L L A M E R I C A N · O N O
R E Y · C L E E K · F I D O
· · M A S · R Y D E R C U P
· T H E T E E · I V Y · · ·
M O O R · L A R G E · C P A
P G A C H A M P I O N S H I P
S O X · O N S E T · P E N T
· · D O N · A B S E N T · ·
K N I C K E R S · E N D ·
H I L L · A C U T E · E L I
A V E · T A M O S H A N T E R
K E N · A D O R E · D O N N A
I N D · J O N E S · S T A T S
```

71 AFTER JUNIOR

```
D E N T · L A S E R · S E P
A G E R · O L I V E · B O N A
N O T A H B E G A Y · A U D I
· · · P R O A M · A L L I N
C L A S S · D A V I S L O V E
R I B · · E T A · N E D · ·
O Z A K I · G R E E N S · ·
· · T O M M Y A R M O U R ·
· · S H A P E S · X R A Y S
S C I · E L S · · · I I I ·
H U G H R O Y E R · L U N N S
E R N I E · L E M O N · · ·
A T I T · T H I R D P L A C E
R I T A · N A T A L · I S A O
S S E · T H E N I · T I P S
```

10 HISTORY LESSON

```
H O L E _ _ T I P _ _ A S H I M
O P E R A _ H O E _ _ S C O R E
P E T E B R O W N _ _ S H O O T
I N S _ D U R A N T _ _ O F N O
_ _ B U B _ _ _ A D O _ _ _ _ _
_ W I L L I A M S P I L L E R
M E G O _ T H E U S A _ _ O N E
A L O C K _ O S S _ L I N D A
R S T _ Y A M A H A _ D E E R
C H A R L I E S I F F O R D
_ _ H E N _ _ O I L
G A R Y _ T A B O O S _ B A G
A L A M O _ J I M T H O R P E
L I N E D _ A N A _ Y E A R N
L E A S E _ M G R _ R E O S
```

19 THIS PLACE IS A ZOO!

```
A E S O P _ W E A K _ T W A Y
I N A I R _ I S L A _ A O K I
D O G L E G L E F T _ G R I P
A S A _ T I M _ A M P _ M D S
_ _ J O N A S _ A R A B
E A T E R S _ H O N O L U L U
A L I B I _ C A R D _ P R O P
G I G _ A M A T E U R _ N E P
L E E R _ U N T O _ A R E W E
E N R O L L E E _ S N A R E D
_ W O O L _ R O O K S
L E O _ B I T _ D L I _ N E O
I R O N _ G O L D E N B E A R
M A D E _ A T I E _ G R O S S
A S S T _ N E E R _ S A N T O
```

28 CADDYSHACK

```
C A P S _ S P A Y _ F A L D O
A L A W _ T I R E _ D R A I N
M I K E H I C K S _ A R U D E
_ _ E L K _ _ O R I S
M I K E F L U F F C O W A N
A R E S T _ P O R O U S
G I L T _ R E N T _ G A L
I S L E S _ G E D _ S L O M O
C H I _ T A R A _ A T O P
_ E A T E R S _ I D A R E
_ A N D R E W M A R T I N E Z
B L O W _ _ L O C
R I V A L _ M I T C H K N O X
E V E R T _ A S E C _ E N N E
W E L D S _ D O D O _ N E A R
```

37 HOW TO IMPROVE AT GOLF

```
S C O R E _ Z E S T _ S H O P
A L L A N _ E C H O _ T O N O
W E I G H T R O O M _ R O L L
S O N _ A H O L D _ T O K Y O
_ _ I N A _ _ A U K
P R A C T I C E G R E E N
A L O N E _ O L D E N _ R O Y
L A G S _ S W I G S _ A N T E
L I E _ I N A N E _ A R I E S
D R I V I N G R A N G E S
_ C A P _ _ B I O
P A V I N _ S A L E M _ L O U
A L O E _ S I M U L A T O R S
R O T S _ A L E C _ L E V E E
S T E T _ W O N K _ S E E M S
```

45 SKIN DEEP

```
M A T T S . J A N . C H I P S
I D I O T . I R A . H A N O I
T O M L E H M A N . E L D E R
. . I V E . B C D . L I M E .
D U F F E R S . Y A M . A S S
A C R E . B A D . M A N N . .
D O E . I S L A M . Y A W P .
E N D E D . E V A . A B E L L
. N C A A . M I R E S . L E E
. O U R S . S I X . S L A M .
S M U . E U R . A U G U S T A
C U P S . B O N . D I N . . .
A L L A T . S U P E R S K I N
R E E V E . E K E . L E A S E
E S S E X . S E N . S T Y L E
```

54 THE OTHER SIDE

```
H E R O N . M C I . S T A Y .
A R E N A . O M E N . H U G E
B O B C H A R L E S . O R E S
I D I E . C H I . . E R N . .
T E L . S T E V E F L E S C H
. S L O E . . R A M . P H I .
. . F L A . R I D . A R E S .
. P H I L M I C K E L S O N .
N E A T . I M A . S A T . . .
O R R . P G A . . W O L F . .
R U S S C O C H R A N . A O L
. H A S . . E O S . M I R A .
E L E V . L E F T H A N D E D
L O S E . A U T H . H O U S E
S A T S . D R Y . A P P T S .
```

63 THE WINNERS' CIRCLE

```
P I N S . S H O E S . B E A N
G A O L . H O R N E . O N L Y
A N N I K A S O R E N S T A M
. . P E R . A M A . E S P . .
B E T S Y K I N G . N O R T H
A E R O S . G O E S O N . . .
I R O N . T O M . T O T A L S
T I O . S E R I P A K . P I E
S E N I O R . N O R . F R E E
. . O B R I E N . H A I T I .
M A I N E . M E G M A L L O N
A C T . R A P . . O W L . . .
T H E U S W O M E N S O P E N
C O M M . E R N I E . F O R E
H O S P . S T O N Y . F L A T
```

72 OPEN SPACES

```
C U J O . C A R S . T O T E M
U P I N . A T I E . A N O T E
B A L T U S R O L . N E O N S
A T L A N T A . M E D I N A H
. . . P E R . B A B E . . . .
F A R . V O T E . O M E A R A
A S H O E . A L S O . P L O T
S H I N N E C O C K H I L L S
T O N O . N O V A . E C O L E
S T O R E D . E M M A . T E A
. . . . . R O A D . A L E . .
O A K M O N T . O V E R L A P
I L I E D . I N V E R N E S S
L A T T E . M E A N . I T I S
S N E A D . E E L S . E A S T
```

11 WHAT A YEAR!

F	A	D	E	D		S	S	W		M	A	M	A	S
A	R	I	S	E		A	A	H		I	R	A	T	E
N	I	C	K	F	A	L	D	O		A	K	R	O	N
S	A	T		E	R	A		A	T	M		K	P	S
		S	N	E	A	D		H	I	H	O			
R	A	T	E	D		M	I	C	E		I	M	U	S
U	N	I	T	E	D		S	U	B		P	E	P	E
B	I	G		D	I	A	G	R	A	M		A	S	A
I	T	E	M		E	M	U		D	A	R	R	E	N
N	A	R	C		G	A	S	P		K	E	A	T	S
		W	I	F	E		T	A	P	E	D			
M	O	O		O	L	E		R	A	S		H	A	L
C	H	O	I	R		N	I	C	K	P	R	I	C	E
A	N	D	R	E		D	R	E		A	U	D	I	O
N	O	S	E	S		S	A	L		R	E	E	D	S

20 THAT'S MY LPGA EVENT!

A	N	T	I		P	A	P	A		M	A	J	O	R
W	A	R	S		I	T	A	T		A	L	A	D	Y
A	M	Y	A	L	C	O	T	T		R	A	M	O	N
R	E	T	O	O	K		S	I	N	K		I	R	E
E	S	O		A	S	U		R	O	S	I	E		
			U	T	T	E	R		N	F	L			
S	A	V	E	S	P	A	R		M	I	S	A	I	M
I	F	I	D	O		H	A	D		B	E	R	R	A
D	A	N	G	L	E		P	A	L	M	T	R	E	E
		R	C	A		R	A	S	T	A				
		E	R	R	O	R		A	C	C		A	D	A
E	G	G		A	S	A	P		O	R	E	G	O	N
B	L	I	N	K		B	E	T	S	Y	K	I	N	G
B	E	L	I	E		I	S	I	T		E	L	E	E
S	E	L	L	S		C	O	M	E		D	E	A	R

29 THAT'S WHAT THEY CALL ME

S	H	O	R	E		S	H	E		H	O	G	A	N
C	A	P	E	S		H	E	Y		A	M	O	R	E
T	H	E	S	Q	U	I	R	E		T	E	L	L	A
V	A	N	E		P	R	E		M	E	N	D	E	R
		T	H	E	K	I	N	G		E	N	S		
L	E	S	S	O	N		O	R	I	O	N			
E	L	I		A	D	V	I	L		N	O	B	L	E
A	B	L	E	R		I	D	A		C	H	E	E	K
D	A	V	I	D		D	I	N	A	H		A	T	E
		E	N	S	U	E		C	O	N	R	A	D	
F	O	R		V	O	L	C	A	N	O				
R	U	S	S	I	A		O	A	R		T	A	L	K
I	N	C	A	N		L	O	R	D	B	Y	R	O	N
E	C	O	N	O		O	P	T		S	E	I	N	E
D	E	T	E	R		A	S	S		S	T	A	G	E

38 ALL MIXED UP

P	I	N	E		M	U	D		J	A	M	E	S
O	S	I	S		S	O	F	A		A	G	A	P	E
H	A	L	S	U	T	T	O	N		S	O	R	E	R
L	O	S		P	I	E		A	D	O		K	E	A
		K	E	L	L	I		U	N	T	O			
P	O	T	E	N	T		N	O	T		O	M	A	R
A	M	I	N	D		O	D	O	R		M	E	D	O
P	E	G		S	E	R	I	P	A	K		A	D	A
A	G	E	D		S	E	A	S		I	N	R	E	D
S	A	R	A		S	O	N		S	N	E	A	D	S
		W	H	O	A		A	M	I	G	O			
A	T	O		L	Y	E		A	N	O		F	E	M
B	O	O	E	D		N	I	C	K	F	A	L	D	O
A	N	D	R	E		O	A	R	S		L	A	G	S
R	I	S	E	N		S	N	O		I	G	E	T

46 GET A JOB

```
S L A B   C O O K   R I O T S
T E R R   L U R E   A T A R I
O N C E   O R B E   N A K E D
I D E A L S   L A G   S E E
C A D D I E M A S T E R
      A S O F   T R E M O R
  S T A R T E R   A S C A R E
V E A L   S I P   A R E A
I N C O M E   C L U B P R O
A T O N A L   A U N T
    G R E E N S K E E P E R
M C C   S C I   E N G I N E
B E A C H   G R I M   G A D S
A L P H A   H A R P   O N I T
S T E A L   T H A T   N O T S
```

55 THE FAB FOURSOME

```
R A F T S   C H I P S   A D S
A L A M O   H A D A T   C U P
F I X I N G A H O L E   O N A
E C O   E T A L   L O P E Z
R E N T E R     A L I
    I A M T H E W A L R U S
F L I E S   O O P S   O N E
R O W D Y   U P S   A R N I E
E G O   O R E O   B A I T S
D O N T P A S S M E B Y
    P A K   C A S P E R
E J E C T   I S A O   O L E
D U E   I T S O N L Y L O V E
I L L   O U T T A   R I L E D
T I S   S T O O P   S I S S Y
```

64 BORN TO GOLF

```
H O P E   M A J O R   N E A R
O R A L   I N A N E   C I T E
G A R Y P L A Y E R   A G E D
A T T   H A L S   U T A H
N E W   E N O   A N N   T O P
  D O W N   G A L   T H E U S
    H O S   R O D   Y E T I
  T A M M I E G R E E N
B M O C   U R N   S S N
L I N K S   O A R   C A R T
T R Y   R O N   E E R   E R A
    L O I N   I S A O   C A P
D E E P   T I G E R W O O D S
I S M E   A D E A L   F R E E
D E A N   P A T T Y   A D D S
```

73 THE BRITISH OPEN

```
L A Y U P   T I E D   C R O P
E V E R S   A T R A   L E M A
W I L L I E P A R K   A B A G
I L L S   N I L   A R E N A
S A O   T O N Y J A C K L I N
    M O S S   A B E E
I D I O T   L Y E   P R O
T O M M O R R I S S E N I O R
A S P   O O P   V A N C E
    M A T T   S T E P
H E N R Y C O T T O N   U S C
A N A M E   A R E   A S T O
D O D O   J A M E S B R A I D
I L E T   I D E A   E A G L E
T A R O   B A S K   T W E E D
```

12 MADE IN JAPAN

```
K I T E     S P R A T     C H A D
A B E L     Y E A R N     L E V I
N I S S A N O P E N       A R E A
E S T     D O N T S     T S A R S
      S A N         P A S
    T O M M Y N A K A J I M A
P E R U     M O T O R     C O B B
L E D         W A R       O H O
S U E S     L I R A S     C R O W
    P R I M E M I N I S T E R
      M O W         F O R
G R I P S     L O A F S     G I T
R O N S     J U M B O O Z A K I
E L M O     I C I E R     I M E T
G L E N     M A T E D     P E S O
```

21 THE AYES HAVE IT

```
S C U S I     W I N M E     T O P
A R N I E     A R E O N     H M O
W A T E R S K I I N G     R A P
S T I R     T E S L A     H E R E
    S E R T A         C L U E
      A M I I N Y O U R W A Y
P A T     I N T O O     G O O S E
I S O R     S I T U P     N O T A
T I M E D     S I T E S   D O H
H A W A I I A N O P E N
    A D A M         S A I N T
C I T Y     M A R D I     S O I T
A S S     J U L I I N K S T E R
M A O     A N D O N     P A R S E
E O N     Y E A T S     S N E A K
```

30 HOLE OF HORRORS

```
E R I K     E N D     B R E A K
T I M E S     R O O     A O R T A
A C U R A     I N E     R U S T Y
T O P M Y T E E S H O T
      I S O       I A N   T E E
W E N T I N T O T H E P O N D
A V A     T I E R     T U T T I
D E M O     C A R O B     P A R T
D R I L L     I V E S     L E O
L A N D E D I N A B U N K E R
E N G     T O S     O B O
      I T H R E E P U T T E D
D E E R E     A L S     R I O D E
E R R O R     E S P     B O R N E
L E A N S     L E N     N E A R
```

39 MY CUP RUNNETH OVER

```
D A L E     R E I D     K I D S
O P U S     B E R N E     A R U T
L A K E N O N A F L O R I D A
E R E     I S T S     A S S E T
      S T S     L I F T
J U D Y R A N K I N     E L S
A M I N O     O A K S     N E W S
I B E       T R I       T E E
L E G S     C H E N     S P A D E
    R O I     P I N G P U T T E R
      S P A N     A S S
S O U S A     L A V A     S P A
A N N I K A S O R E N S T A M
K I T E     S E C T S     A I R Y
E N O S     A C H Y     P R E S
```

47 FOR THE BIRDS

```
A P O P . S T I R . B E A S T
N I N O . N O N O . U M B E R
D U C K H O O K S . S C O R E
I S E E M . . B I G . . I V E
. . D O U B L E E A G L E S .
B O B . S L O . O N A . . . .
A M O K . G E T A . T U R B O
J A Y H A A S . B U Z Z A R D
A N D A S . S P I N . E G A D
. K I A . E D U . S Y S . . .
R O B I N F R E E M A N . . .
A L L . C A L . G I V E S . .
I D A H O . G O O S E N E C K
N I K O N . E U R O . T R O Y
S E E P S . S T E W . H A N S
```

56 IN LAST PLACE

```
F L A G . B A D . S P A S
B E L O W . O S I S . H E L P
I T A L O . O A T H . E L L A
. F U Z Z Y Z O E L L E R .
T O P . L E E . V A L E N S
S N E A D S . D U E S . T S E
K E R M I T Z A R L E Y . .
S O T O . O N S . O L D E
. B A B E Z A H A R I A S
P I P . W A S A . I S E E I T
I N A C A N . E L S . U S A
L A R R Y Z I E G L E R . .
O B O E . A N D Y . T I G E R
T I L E . I T U P . S C O R E
S T E P . O C T . H A R D
```

65 THE HOLE TRUTH

```
T I P O F F . E A R S . D O C
O M E A R A . A L A W . U F O
G O L F I S A G A M E . T A R
A N T . T I L . D A R L A
. W H E R E T H E B A L L
M O T H E R . A O N E
A F R O S . C O P E . L I E S
T A I . A D O R E R S . N R A
A N O N . A C E S . E A T I N
. O S L O . S T R O K E
P O O R L Y A N D T H E
A L A M O . O O O . D O S
V I R . P L A Y E R S W E L L
I V E . E X P O . M A R C I A
N E D . D I E U . S P Y I N G
```

74 G'DAY, AMERICA!

```
M E C C A . E L O N . C A R T
A T L A S . X E N A . A L T O
T H E T H R E E A U S S I E S
T E E . E A R . T A T
E L K I N G T O N . G R A D Y
A S S N . S U E S . O B O E
. C H I . T R E E . L E T
W H O V E W O N T H E
I T E . T A R A . T A E
T W I G . N A I L . A G E S
S A R A H . S T A Y S T R U E
. R A N . D O A . A N E
P G A C H A M P I O N S H I P
A N T I . M A R E . T R A C E
Y U M A . E G O S . A I M E D
```

13 ALL-AMERICAN BOYS

```
W A C K O . L O C A L . . B A Y
O T H E R . O R O N O . . A L A
O R A L R O B E R T S . . N O R
D A I . . M O O N . . T O K E N
S P R A I N . . . A M O R . . .
. . . B R I G H A M Y O U N G .
I W A L K . R O D S . . . P O L
S E L E S . A S A . L A T T E .
L I L . . S T E P . I B S E N .
A R I Z O N A S T A T E . . . .
. . G I R L . . . N E L S O N .
S H A P E . S P O T . . E N E .
H O T . G E O R G I A T E C H .
O N O . O G L E R . T O M E I .
P E R . N O O S E . M E S A S .
```

22 TIGER CATCHING

```
. S T R A P . W O W S . . A F T
S T E A L A . E R O O . . M I R
L E E W E S T W O O D . . A V E
I W O . S O H O . D A R R E N .
D E F S . . A N A . . B E I T .
E D F I O R I . M A E S T R O .
. . . S L O . P O H L . T O N .
. P H I L M I C K E L S O N . .
S A O . I A N S . R E T . . . .
P R U D E N T . D O N A T E S .
I T S A . L I E . . Y A N K . .
T H E M E S . N C A A . L E I .
I R S . T H O M A S B J O R N .
N E A . C O R E . S L A N G S .
G E T . H O R N . N E W S Y . .
```

31 IN THE BEGINNING

```
. B A R R . R O Y S . . S H S .
A R N I E . E X E C S . . H O P
K I N G J A M E S I I . . A L A
I T I S . T A N . . N I K E S .
D A K . A L I . S T E V E . . .
. . A L B A N Y N E W Y O R K .
. . E L S . O I L . . . F E E .
E M P T Y . C U P . L O F T Y .
A P R . . F A R . S Y S . . . .
T H E S I L V E R C L U B . . .
. . J A M I E . I R E . L A D .
S A U N A . E V A . B A S E .
O L D . G U T T A P E R C H A .
D E G . E R R O L . R A K E D .
A X E . L E N S . A S S N .
```

40 HAIL TO THE CHIEF

```
B U S H . P A I L . . D A N E
O S L O . A T S E A . . E V E N
B O O N . G E R A L D F O R D .
. . . C H E N . F L A . I V E .
H O O H A . . . E R O D E D .
A R N O L D P A L M E R . . .
S I T . F O R C E . D A V I D
P O H L . T I T A N . L E D A .
S N E A D . C O S T S . R I N .
. . P E T E R T H O M S O N .
L O O P E R . . . S E E M Y .
A P R . R E A . T H O R . .
K E N V E N T U R I . I O W A
E R O O . D I V O T . O P E N .
S A T S . T A D S . N A T O .
```

92

48 WHO SAID THAT?

```
D A N A   W A S H     A B A T
A M O S   H A L E     L I M O
H A N K A A R O N   A L L O N
    A L T O     R I V A L R Y
B R A   L O N     I S O   Y E S
R E L I E F       S N U G
I N A N Y     T H O U     P R O S
T O N O   M A I N E     N A P A
A S S N   A P T S     C O H E N
    H E R R       R E W A R D
I K E   I D O   M O L   M A Y
T O P S P I N     A B E L
I R A T E     Y O G I B E R R A
S A R A     O P E N     T E A M
A N D Y     U S E S     S O N Y
```

57 V-J DAY

```
H I N D I     F I J I     T R A P
O N E A L   O N E S     R U N A
R O O K I E O F T H E Y E A R
I N N   E S T O     E M B
Z E S T     P E R M   M A Y E R
      W I N D     I T A     A A A
S E M I S     U N O     A C T S
P G A C H A M P I O N S H I P
O G R E   R E S     P U T T S
T O I   G T E   G A R R
S N A K E   T R E S     E I N E
      A N O   Y O K E     R O T
P O N T E V E D R A B E A C H
U H O H   A L E G     B A T H E
T O N Y   L I R E     S T E E L
```

66 SWINGING STARS

```
P R O A M   A T T       E D G E
R A N G E   R I O   T E A R S
A M Y A L C O T T   E L V E S
M A X   O N L O A N     I T E
      E R N I E E L S   D A N
L A W S O N       L E A D
A R I S E   T I M E   D U M B
D E L A   T W A I N   O V E R
D A L Y   R O N S   C R A T E
      I S E E     T H E L O T
A L E   S A M S N E A D
D O W   I T A L I A     A S K
I R O N S   M E G M A L L O N
M E O U T   A P E   F A L D O
E N D S   S T L   T W I S T
```

75 A MAJOR PLAYER

```
A P E     T H A W     S L I P
L O U D   H O L E S   I A M A
S H R E V E P O R T   X M E N
  L O U I S I A N A S T A T E
      S E A   D E L A Y
A R G   S U N   R E L   M E N
C O R D   R O B     S A U D I
Q U A D C I T Y C L A S S I C
U N D E R   E A U   H E C K
A D S   E W E   B C D   S T S
      K E I T H   K O S
B U I C K C H A L L E N G E
U S G A   K E M P E R O P E N
D E E R   S L U G S   B A L E
S A T S   S P A S   S S W
```

14 MM NUMBERS

```
AMY . BRAD . FAXON
DOA . IOWA . SERENE
JOHNDALY . ALFRED
. ODD SELLS .
CAMRY . ITS . HOP
ADAM . LAWNS . PORE
BOY . HERO . ARUBA
. FREDCOUPLES .
BEACH . DROP . TRI
ASIA . WASNT . GOON
TAR . TAN . FONDA
. KITNA . PAL
FRINGE . FREDFUNK
CAREER . ROPE . SEE
CHEER . OWES . STY
```

23 CORRECT, CORRECT, CORRECT!

```
DAS . SKIDS . JONES
OCT . AESOP . UBOAT
WHOWONTWO . METRE
NEWS . SOUP . ATV
. USOPENSINTHE
AMI . EUR . SONO
NINETIES . TRAP
TENDS . PED . TRYBA
SNOW . ERNIEELS
. IBIS . ARE . SYS
PAYNESTEWART
ATA . HUEY . ECHO
VERVE . LEEJANZEN
INDIA . MORAN . ART
NOSED . ONEND . ROO
```

32 PGA CHAMPIONSHIP TALE

```
VIJAY . TOMS . ISAY
OMAHA . APIE . DECA
WANAMAKERTROPHY
STS . MEN . ANTES
. ABET . ABIT
WALTERHAGEN . ARK
AGAIN . DETS . LEE
TAYE . SLASH . ROLL
EMU . ATOP . MAHAL
REP . LEFTINATAXI
. CAPT . TAPS
IBEAM . ORR . IDE
DETROITMICHIGAN
LENT . NINE . ITOLD
ERAS . AMID . MARYS
```

41 THE SHOT

```
BEARD . LED . JOB
INDIA . SEGER . AVE
DOUBLEEAGLE . NET
ELL . LINKS . GOERS
SAT . AGTS . PAUL
. ASH . WRITER
SPAN . TCCHEN . AOL
HOLDA . OOO . STRAY
SOB . BOBMAY . EYRE
. HARRIS . ACE
TOIL . TELL . STP
FIRED . ORATE . IRA
ADO . GENESARAZEN
RES . EVENT . KNEES
RAS . EST . SASSY
```